The Old Red Shirt

T R A N S M O N T A N U S   1 2

Published by New Star Books
Series Editor: Terry Glavin

Other books in the Transmontanus series

The Old Red Shirt

PIONEER POETS OF BRITISH COLUMBIA

Yvonne Mearns Klan

TRANSMONTANUS | NEW STAR BOOKS VANCOUVER

Dedicated to Sandi and Julian,
Teresa and Celeste, and to Peter,
without whose love and encouragement
these poems would still be lying
in the bottom of a drawer

Acknowledgments

Most of the poems in this collection are in the public domain. The author has made every effort to track down the descendents of those other poets who died after December 31, 1948, and thanks the estate of Bertrand Sinclair, which granted permission to reprint "The Bank Trollers," and the estate of Earl Pollon, which granted permission to reprint "The Astronomer." All remaining poems are used with thanks to the poets and their families.

Thanks are due to many people who helped me find information on now-obscure authors and publications — information which would add interest to the poems, but which was not readily available. The ever-obliging staff of the North Vancouver District Library (Lynn Valley) rendered patient assistance as did the staff in Special Collections of the Vancouver Public Library. I'm particularly grateful to Jack M. for his interest and encouragement.

Others who assisted in "getting it right" were Danielle Arcand, Suzette Bahar, Susan Buss, Kathleen Dalzell, Anne Holt, Martin Kyllo, Greg Nesteroff, Bill Quackenbush and Jim Shaw.

A Tapestry of Vanished Voices

The Cariboo miner trudges back to his solitary cabin after a hard and mostly unfruitful shift at the diggings. Grimy and worksore, he fires up the woodstove and heats a simple supper: fatback, beans, and bannock, his customary Spartan fare. Afterwards, in the glow of the coal-oil lamp, he sips strong tea, lights his pipe, and dreams fitfully of unfound gold. Then he reaches for a grubby notebook, a stub of pencil, and begins, laboriously, to work on an unfinished poem. The words come slowly but he perseveres. At length he finishes the poem, reads what he has written and feels a small glow of accomplishment.

Curiously enough, the writing of poetry was a fairly common activity among British Columbia's pioneers with even a smattering of education. Writing filled the need for self-expression otherwise lacking in their humdrum and hardscrabble lives. Predictably, much of this poetry was naïve, sentimental doggerel, unfit for any sort of publication. But there were a fair number of unique exceptions. These exceptions provide the substance and backbone of this unusual collection

Yvonne Klan, writer, ardent history buff, and dogged researcher, came across these forgotten verses while delving through various archives for other material. They proliferated in the pages of historic newspapers and such long-defunct magazines as *Westward Ho* and *B.C. Digest*. They also appeared in a variety of small, self-published, and marginally circulated chapbooks. Fascinated, she began to collect the best of them for her own enjoyment.

Over the years, these pioneer poems accumulated in Yvonne's files and she began to toy with the idea of compiling them in a book. Her original concept involved combining them with prose pieces. She assembled a tentative manuscript and showed it to an editor. The editor demurred on the grounds that the collection lacked focus. Yvonne shelved the idea for a time and went on to other projects.

These projects all demanded research, and Yvonne began to turn up more and more poems of historic interest. Once again she began to think in terms of a book but this time she would use only the poems, accompanied by original introductions and footnotes. She arranged the poems in roughly chronological order and subject matter. A definite structure began to emerge.

The Old Red Shirt is a remarkable book. A historical mosaic, it touches many bases presenting British Columbia's past from the point of view of the people who actually lived the events. A few of these people are relatively well known. Bertrand W. Sinclair, for example, was a highly successful novelist in the 1920s and 1930s. When his work fell out of fashion, he became a commercial fisherman, based at Pender Harbour, and penned *The Bank Trollers*, a dramatic ode to that profession.

Walter Moberly, the most famous of BC's early surveyors and the discoverer of the Eagle Pass through the Rockies, wrote poetry and was also the subject of poems such as a very offbeat ditty titled *The Rape of the Boot*:

> Intrepid Walter Moberly had many a vicissitude
> exploring in the Rockies and through the Cariboo.
> Right well he knew the dangers and he exercised
>   solicitude
> as far as it was possible, to obviate them too . . .

The poem goes on to describe a situation both funny and bizarre.

While humour is certainly not lacking in this book, it is counterpointed by serious themes. Lloyd Roberts (son of poet Charles G.D. Roberts) shows evidence of having inherited his father's skill in *The Fruit Rancher*:

He sees the rosy apples cling like flowers on the bough;
He plucks the purple plums and spills the cherries on the
  grass;
He wanted peace and silence — God gives him plenty
  now
His feet upon the mountain and his shadow on the pass . . .

While most of the writers in this anthology are, to say the least, obscure, that is certainly not to denigrate their contributions. Their degree of skill varies but all of them have something valid to impart. They bring to life long-forgotten characters and incidents that would otherwise be totally lost. George Winkler, known as "the prospector poet," conjures up two stalwarts of the past in *On the West Kettle River Road*. It ends on a poignant note:

The peaceful flowing river winds
The stately spruces through
And few remain of olden times
That Gorman's hostel knew.

Now motor cars the roads infest
And strangers speed their ways
But Father Pat and Gorman West
Belong to other days.

(Father Pat, known as the miners' priest, also appears in a poem of his own.)

The poems in *The Old Red Shirt* range widely through the BC backcountry of distant years. They move back and forth between drama and comedy with many stops in between. What knits them all together is Yvonne's astute commentary on each piece. She sketches in the background of the poem in question and, wherever possible, provides a thumbnail sketch of the author. Her informed introductions and footnotes weave the otherwise disparate verses into a dazzling tapestry of bygone days. *The Old Red Shirt* is a valuable addition to the canon of BC historical writing. It is also a stimulating and highly enjoyable read.

PETER TROWER

JANUARY 2004

Contents

Medicine Man, Queen Charlotte Islands.

BC ARCHIVES NO. E-03013

Caribou Medicine Song[1]

I need your help, O caribou.
Come swiftly to me.
You see I have laid my hands on the
   sufferer.
Come and lay your hoofs where I have
   laid my hands.

I need your help.
Without your help there is no healing
   in my hands today.
Come so quickly that your tail stands
   erect.

— TRADITIONAL

In the early days, British Columbia's First Peoples understood that there were maladies white doctors could not cure. The sufferer's only hope of relief was to seek the help of a medicine man, whose power usually had come to him in a dream. With drumming, rattle shaking, and singing, the power was prevailed upon to help effect a cure.

For a long time Tyee David of Hagwilget had been plagued by animal spirits — bears, dogs, wolves — invading his body. It was a sickness no white doctor could cure so he asked medicine men Alex Tyee and Donald Grey to extricate the bothersome bear spirit that had lodged itself in his throat. On the night of January

---

1. Jenness Diamond. *The Sekani Indians of British Columbia*. Bulletin No. 84 (Ottawa: National Museum of Canada, 1937). p. 77.

9, 1931, Alex and Donald arrived at Tyee David's house. The patient, wearing a bearskin cloak and a headdress of eagle feathers, knelt in the centre of the room. Beside him, Alex drummed while Donald shook a carved rattle. Well-wishers thronged the room to help out with chanting and to witness the medicine men scoop the evil spirit out of Tyee David's body and blow it away.

Unfortunately, the healing ceremony was being witnessed by two RCMP officers who were spying through Tyee David's window. They brought the proceedings to an abrupt close and charged the medicine men under section 443 of the Criminal Code: "Everyone is guilty of an indictable offence and liable to one year's imprisonment who pretends to exercise or use any kind of witchcraft, sorcery, enchantment or conjuration."

It did no good to point out to the judge that the medicine men had not been "pretending," that their treatment had successfully dislodged the bear spirit and cured the patient. Donald Grey and Alex Tyee were each given a one-year suspended sentence.[2] A new Criminal Code, introduced in 1953, contained no mention of witchcraft.

John Clarke (1781–1852) began his fur trading career with the North West Company. He was handsome, arrogant, charming, daring, and quick to the sword — a true Lord of the North. A fellow officer commented, "The first brush or onset of Clarke is irresistible. No servant will attempt to disobey his orders, and few Indians can resist his entreaties. He cajoles, condoles, and seems to command every string that can touch the heart of a Canadian."[3] "Canadians" were the North West Company voyageurs who came from Quebec. The Hudson's Bay Company (HBC) recruited workers from Britain; thus, the firm and its employees were commonly called "the English."

In 1809, when he was in charge of Fort St. John,[4] the banks of

2. *The Province*, March 25, 1931.
3. E. E. Rich, ed. *Colin Robertson's Correspondence Book* (Toronto: Champlain Society for Hudson's Bay Record Society, 1939), p. 61.
4. W. K. Lamb, ed. *Sixteen Years in the Indian Country. The Journal of Daniel William Harmon* (Toronto: Macmillan, 1957).

the Peace River resounded as he led his voyageurs in singing his favourite paddling song. Clarke's daughter describes the scene: "Raising their paddles high in the air for the first dip, they gave a parting call, and like an arrow the canoe shot out into the current, the crew singing."

Paddling Song[5]

Ou irons-nous,   *(Where will we)*
La ridondaine!   *(Tra-la-la)*
Çe soir coucher?   *(Sleep tonight?)*
La ridondé.   *(Tra-la-la)*

Ou irons-nous çe soir coucher?
Ou irons-nous çe soir coucher?

A la maison   *(At home)*
La ridondaine!
Accoutumé   *(As usual)*
La ridondé!

A la maison accoutumé
A la maison accoutumé

Et nous aurons!   *(And we shall have)*
La ridondaine!
De quoi souper   *(Something to eat)*
La ridondé!

Et nous aurons de quoi souper
Et nous aurons de quoi souper.

Le lendemain   *(The next day)*
La ridondaine!
A déjeuner   *(At breakfast)*
La ridondé

Le lendemain à déjeuner
Le lendemain à déjeuner
    — TRADITIONAL

Once the brigades arrived in New Caledonia the singing, rollicking voyageur was transformed into a grumbling, wretched pack animal, transporting trading goods and salmon from post to post by dog sled or backpack. Pemmican, his favorite staple, was no longer available. It was replaced by salmon — dried, indigestible, and often scarce — with an occasional feast of dog meat. Working conditions were so miserable that the Hudson's Bay Company was obliged to pay higher wages in New Caledonia than in

5. Adele Clarke. *Old Montreal* (Montreal: The Herald Publishing Co., 1906).

any other part of the country.

La Derante was one of the voyageurs who packed loads between Fraser Lake and Ft. St. James. On February 25, 1823 the clerk at Fraser Lake noted "La Derante . . . is so much reduced that I could not refuse his earnest request to be allowed to remain here today, but he is to start tomorrow morning with a load of 180 salmon. He is so weak that he does not think he will be able, with his small dogs, to get up the hills. I therefore send Old Joseph along with him." On February 28th, La Derante arrived at Fort St. James with his 180 salmon but, recorded the clerk, "[he] is so very much emaciated and reduced that I scarcely knew him, tears came to his Eyes when he spoke to me, and I could not find it in my heart to send him back without allowing him some repose." The repose was short. On March 2nd, he arrived at Fraser Lake with his load and prepared for next morning's return trip. The clerk noted that he was "in such a wretched condition . . ." I gave him [the lighter] load of salmon as he would not be able to keep up with the others."[6]

Song of the Voyageurs[7]

In the course of the journey,
Subject to sudden mishaps,
Your body soaked to the bone,
Woken before dawn by the birds;
With no rest,
neither night nor day,
With nothing but wearisome work,
Always worrying about the approach of
   winter
and being beaten by the winds. . . .

Oh! I tell you, comrades,
There is no one on earth
Who endures as much misery as we do
who are married to our work
As for me, I can't wait
until we get home again,
Never again will I come
to this damned country
which has almost worn me out.
                    — TRADITIONAL

---

6. B.188/a/1 and B.188/b/2.   7. Brian Davis, ed. *The Poetry*   (Toronto: NC Press, 1976).
HBC Archives.   *of the Canadian People*

When gold was discovered on the Queen Charlotte Islands and the mainland, miners from California flocked northward, and Governor James Douglas was faced with the enormous responsibility of maintaining British law and order, regulating mining claims, providing transportation routes, and laying out new towns. To assist him, Britain's Colonial Secretary sent out a body of Royal Engineers. One group boarded the *Thames City* in October 1858, sailed via Cape Horn, and arrived at Esquimalt six months later.[8] They published the *Emigrant Soldiers' Gazette* and *Cape Horn Chronicle*, from which this poem is taken.

A Farewell Ditty[9]

A Ship once sailed on a voyage long,
With six score soldiers stout and strong,
With married women thirty-one,
Thirty-four children plump and young.
October the ninth they came on board,
October the tenth the Pilot roared
"All hands up anchor!" and off they go
To the tune of the sailors "ho heigh
    ho!" . . .

So they sailed along did this goodly
    crew,
Some sick, some seedy, some white,
    some blue;
By and by, however they all got right;

A paper they had each Saturday night,
Afterwards songs in the moon's pale
    light;
And oft would they dwell on their
    prospects bright
In Columbia land, their destination,
With its mines of gold for the English
    nation.
Christmas day they spent at sea,
And made themselves jolly as jolly
    could be;
Three days after they made the land,
And soon the Pilot's steady hand
Steered them safe into Stanley Port,
For fear they should ere long fall short

---

8. For an account of the Royal Engineers see Beth Hill's *Sappers: The Royal Engineers in British Columbia* (Victoria: Horsdal & Schubart, 1987). Charles Wilson, Royal Engineer, also kept an entertaining record of his experiences in British Columbia. See George F. G. Stanley, ed. *Mapping the Frontier: Charles Wilson's Diary of the Survey of the 49th Parallel, 1858-1862* (Toronto: Macmillan, 1970). 9. *Emigrant Soldiers' Gazette* and *Cape Horn Chronicle.* Vancouver Public Library, Special Collections.

Of water — fifteen days spent here,
Where provisions of all sorts were
	horribly dear.
Heigh, heigh, ho! they're off again
To the horrible cold and the pelting
	rain,
And the wind, and the sea, and every ill
Of Cape Horn's dreary regions, till
In 40° South the weather became
Mild, and fine, and jolly again.
Four days then in Valparaiso,
Where, it's quite true, though I'm sorry
	to say so,
They can't find anything better to do
Than squabble and kick up a hullabaloo.
Off again on St. Valentine's day;
They crossed the Equator, so they say,
On the sixth of March, and, doubt it
	who may,
No one got drunk on St. Patrick's day.
At length a chap, said to be witty,
Thought he would write a farewell
	ditty,
So when 17,000 miles they'd run,
And all were happy and full of fun,
He determined to pay his farewell debt
To the dying *Emigrant Soldiers'*
	Gazette,
And, when scarce 500 miles from the
	harbour,
Thus commenced his long palaver;
Farewell to the cold and freezing blast,
The bursting sail and quivering mast;
While foam-capp'd waves defy the gale
We'll snugly sip our foam-capped ale.
Farewell "head winds" and "quarter
	breezes,"

Each puff may come from whence it
	pleases;
Farewell to Cape Horn's cold and wet,
Farewell the tropics' sun and sweat,
Farewell the fok'sle, waist and poop,
Farewell thick biscuit and thin pea
	soup,
Farewell the suet, grog, and junk,
One was weak, the others stunk.
Farewell to the hen-coop and lonely
	duck,
Farewell to Long-boat Square and
	muck,
Farewell to Laundry Lane and Galleys,
We'll cook our grub in glades and val-
	leys.
Farewell to sheets, and spars, and sails,
Farewell to dolphins, sharks, and
	whales,
Farewell to the rigging, farewell to the
	decks,
Farewell to the hatch where we've nigh
	broke our necks,
Farewell to the dove-cot, farewell to the
	bugs,
And the noises that every night sound
	in our lugs.[10]
Farewell to the cabin, farewell to the
	goose,
Farewell to the pantry and steward's
	caboose,
Farewell to the hammocks, farewell to
	the clews,
Farewell to the would-be Irish stews,
Farewell to cockroaches and thieving
	cats,
And a long farewell to those horrible rats,

---

10. "Lugs" is an old British term for ears.

That screech and quarrel every night,
And make one shudder and feel in a
   fright.
Farewell to parades with bared necks
   and feet,
Farewell to the lime-juice that's hardly
   sweet,
Farewell to the water of rusty hue,
Farewell to the *Abstract of Progress* too;
Farewell to our everlasting view

Of cloudy sky and ocean blue,
Farewell to the Petrel's warning note,
Farewell to our dreary life afloat;
I've three good hearty farewells yet:
Farewell to the *Emigrant Soldiers'*
   Gazette,
A long farewell to the old *Thames City,*
Farewell at last to my farewell ditty.

    — THE ROYAL ENGINEERS

During US President (1845–49) James Polk's election campaign, he demanded that Britain cede Oregon to the United States and had set in motion events that led to Texas entering the Union in December 1845, followed by California in 1850. Though his "54–40 or fight" slogan became a rallying cry, he settled for the 1846 Treaty of Washington compromise, which placed the US-Canada boundary at the 49th parallel. In 1852, California miners learned that gold was found in the Queen Charlottes and sailed north to the new Eldorado. Governor Douglas feared they would colonize the islands and annex them to the US. If this were indeed their intent, hostile natives and a British warship anchored nearby caused them to rethink the matter and return south. Six years later, when news of Fraser River's gold reached San Francisco, California miners again left their played-out diggings and swarmed northward. Though Polk was now out of office, his sentiments remained popular and found expression in many newspapers, including the Olympia, WA *Pioneer and Democrat.*

Hurrah, Boys, The River's Ours[11]

Up above, among the mountains,
Men have found the golden fountains;
Seen where they flow! Oh joy transcen-
dent!
Down, down, in noiseless streams
transplendent,
Then, hurrah, and set your riggings —
Sail above, to richer diggings.

When news gets where Buch and Cass
is,[12]
Johnny Bull can go where grass is —

He may rave and rant to foaming,
It will never stop our coming.
Then, hurrah, nor wait for papers,[13]
The license men may cut their capers.

Soon our banner will be streaming,
Soon the eagle will be screaming,
And the lion — see it cowers,
Hurrah, boys, the river's ours.
Then, hurrah, nor wait for calling,
For the Frazer's river falling.

— ANONYMOUS

Among BC's early pathfinders, Walter Moberly, Civil Engineer, (1832–1859), best known as the discoverer of the Canadian Pacific Railroad's (CPR) Eagle Pass route through the Rockies, is one of the most colourful. English born, he came to Canada in 1854. In Toronto, he met artist Paul Kane, who had journeyed to the Pacific Northwest in 1847 and had made numerous sketches of Aboriginal life. Moberly recalled, "I was almost daily in his studio or house. . . . His description of the Pacific coast . . . interested me very much . . . and I decided to go there."[14] Moberly arrived in BC in 1858, surveyed lots for New Westminster, and explored Burrard Inlet with Robert Burnaby. In 1859, while exploring between Yale and Lytton to determine the feasibility of blasting a wagon road through the Fraser River canyons, a strange incident occurred.

11. Olympia *Pioneer and Democrat,* November, 1858, quoted in Willard E. Ireland, "British Columbia's American Heritage," *Annual Report* (Toronto: Canadian Historical Association, 1948), p. 70.

12. US President James Buchanan and his Secretary of State, Lewis Cass.
13. A reference to Governor Douglas's proclamation that all gold found on the Fraser and Thompson belonged to the Crown and to his institution of mining licenses.
14. See Moberly's autobiography, *The Rocks and Rivers of British Columbia* (London: H. Blacklock, 1885).

The Rape of the Boot

Intrepid Walter Moberly had many a vicissitude
exploring in the Rockies and through the Cariboo.
Right well he knew the dangers and he exercised solicitude,
as far as it was possible, to obviate them too.

Walter
Moberly
had many
adventures

He met with weird adventures, remarkable and numerous,
far more than are vouchsafed to the ordinary chap;
and some were spiced with danger, some gay and others
    humorous
but his spirit never faltered whatever the mishap.

He encountered savage grizzlies and the deadly rattlesnake
and he backed bucking bronchos and rode them on the trail.
Wild Indians could not scare him nor "bad whites" his courage
    shake,
the Sheriff served a writ on him and then he did not quail.

He had taken the first contract for the road to Cariboo.
His men went off and left the work to join the search for gold.
The Government would not pay him the monies that were due
and cancelled his road contract with loss to him untold.

He could have fled the country and left every obligation,
but that was not his nature, although these were large and many;
and it took him eight long, scrimping years to win emancipation.
He was able then to liquidate and paid them every penny.[15]

but this
concerns
an encounter
with a pig

To go into that deeply here is not in my indenture.
It were a striking subject, a theme inspiring, big;
but the aim of this slight ditty is to set out an adventure
that befell this hardy pioneer pertaining to a pig.

---

15. Moberly details his financial difficulties in "History of the Cariboo Road" in *Art, Historical and Scientific Association, Session 1907–08. Historical Papers* (Vancouver: Clarke & Stewart).

He arrives at
Chapman's
Bar

Once when travelling down the Fraser in his work of exploration
one evening tired and footsore he arrived at Chapman's Bar.
There was none to bid him welcome but he asked no invitation
to make himself at once at home for he had travelled far.

and after
dining

It was hot and he was thirsty but he found some handy food there
and with flapjacks and with
bacon he soon cooked himself a dinner;
and, washed down with fragrant coffee, he adjudged it very good
    fare
for any old campaigner whether he were saint or sinner.

he lies
down
to sleep

There was a new log building with no doors or windows in it
where a stretcher made of gunny sacks invited him to sleep.
So he threw himself upon it and was "fast" in half a minute
and knew no more till morning when the dawn began to peep.

In the
morning he
is awakened
by a pig

Then to his waking consciousness there came a curious snorting
and a grunting loud and dissonant just close beside his head.
So he opened wide his eyes in time to see a pig cavorting
naively round the premises and nuzzling at his bed.

He throws
his boot
at the
animal

In an instant he had raised himself annoyed by such intrusion
and looked around for something to rap the porker's snout.
Then he picked up his boot in the heat of his confusion
and threw it at the grunting beast with hope to drive it out.

but to his
chagrin the
pig made
away with it

In this he was successful but, much to his astonishment,
the pig "pinched" the missile and quickly made escape;
nor waited to listen to the traveller's admonishment,
who followed in his stockinged feet indignant at the rape.

"His pigship" proved the swifter and vanished in the thicket
before poor Walter Moberly could catch him by the tail;
and sadly he soliloquized, "Now that just wasn't 'cricket,'
to steal my boot away from me when I must walk to Yale!"

So the
explorer
had to walk
to Yale with
but one boot.

'T was a twenty-five mile journey without any road to follow
and it proved a painful penance for his bruised and bleeding
    foot;[16]
but by nightfall he espied with joy the town's lights in the hollow
    where he sojourned to recuperate and bought another boot.

— UNKNOWN

Walter Moberly — impulsive, stubborn, and lacking business acu-
men — was undoubtedly a trial to work with, but the enmity he
could engender was more than matched by the deep friendships
he formed. Moberly wrote extensively and sometimes turned his
hand to poetry.[17]

We just shake hands at meeting
With many that come nigh
We nod the head in greeting
To many that go by —

But welcome through the gateway
Our few old friends and true;
Then hearts leap up and straightway
There open house for you, old friends,
There's open house for you . . .

— WALTER MOBERLY

Well-travelled, well-read, and a congenial companion, he treas-
ured his wide circle of friends.

The fragrant perfume that yet may
    cling
To some small flower sweet and fair,
The strain harmonious that may bring
The echo of some once-loved air;

A sudden thought, a dream, a prayer
That come, divine it we cannot,
And mem'ry will responsive flare;
A friend once made is ne'er forgot.

— WALTER MOBERLY

16. "I managed to find the
worn-out foot of a miner's
discarded boot . . . but as it
was too big I packed moss
and leaves around my foot."

Walter Moberly, *Reminis-
cences*. Vancouver City
Archives.
17. For Moberly's biography
see Noel Robinson's *Blazing*

*the Trail Through the Rockies:
The Story of Walter Moberly*
(Vancouver: 1915, n.p.).

While Moberly was happily blazing wilderness trails and exploring whatever lay "beyond," his sister, Emma, mourned his absence.

Invitation to Return Home[18]

Come home! There is a sorrowing
  breath
In music since ye went,
And the early flower-scents wander by
With mournful memories blent.
The tones in every household voice
Are grown more sad and deep;
And the sweet word — "brother" —
  wakes a wish
To turn aside and weep.

Oh ye beloved! come home! — The
  hour
Of many a greeting tone,
The time of hearth-light and of song
Returns — and ye are gone;
And darkly, heavily it falls
On the forsaken coomb,
Burdening the heart with tenderness,
That deepens midst the gloom.

Where finds it you, ye wandering one!
With all your boyhood's glee
Untamed? Beneath the desert's palm,
Or on the lone mid-sea?
By stormy hills of battles old?
Or where dark rivers foam?
Oh! life is dim where ye are not —
Back, ye beloved, come home!

Come with the leaves and winds of
  spring,
And swift birds, o'er the main!
Our love has grown too sorrowful —
Bring us its youth again!
Bring the glad tone to music back!
Still, still your home is fair,
The spirit of your sunny life
Alone is wanting there.
      — EMMA B. MOBERLY

At the bottom of Emma's poem Walter wrote

Answer, W. to E.

A restless spirit, a ceaseless wish
Debars one from a home of bliss.
      — W. M.

---

18. Moberly fonds. Vancouver City Archives.

Walter Moberly
BC ARCHIVES A-01814

Walter Moberly died in 1912 harbouring a deep bitterness towards the CPR who, he felt, had treated him unfairly. His friends concurred and when he died several of them composed poetic epitaphs in which they mention the injustice.

Tribute to Walter Moberly[19]

Rugged and rough was the mortal career
Of the engineer who lies buried here;
His heart never failed; his nerve never trembled
When through the mountains of B.C. he scrambled,
Before political wind-bags assembled.

Now many may talk of the old Pioneers
Of British Columbia but few will shed tears

---

19. Add. Ms. 33, Moberly fonds. Vancouver City Archives.

For the man who devoted his best years
To develop the country for his compeers
And enable its revenue to pay up arrears.

He spent many years to ensure cheap transportation
For the people of the great Canadian nation.
When aged seventy-five he sought compensation
From the rich CPR to avoid starvation
And his worldly affairs going to damnation.

His appeal was in vain, it was treated with scorn
Which he learnt by a letter from Sir William Van Horne.
The grand silent mountains will always remind
The traveller who the wanting link did find.
And thus the Palliser-Moberly route was defined.

For when Palliser said there was no way
To lay the track for Britain's sway
Then Moberly took the work in hand
And secured for the nation the iron band
That makes a great and prosperous land.

       — HIS OLDEST FRIEND

No one knows how many lives were lost in the stampede to the Fraser River gold fields. Men perished in river torrents or were murdered by the natives or fellow miners. New Westminster's *British Columbian* recorded many of these events. "Hudson's Bay Company officers were confident there would be no trouble if the miners refrained from selling the Indians whiskey and did not meddle with their women; good advice which the whites did not follow. . . . The morning light disclosed the headless bodies of two white men on the river brink. Later in the day three more decapitated bodies floated down stream."[20] One adventurer was haunted by a

20. D. W. Higgins, "The Battle of Spuzzum," in *The*   *Mystic Spring and Other Tales of Western Life*   (Toronto: Briggs, 1904).

tragedy he witnessed when a canoe full of men swirled into the Fraser's rapids. "Their canoe had been half-filled by the breakers. We saw them drifting helplessly, broadside on, and as they neared the whirlpool they lifted their hands and shrieked aloud. . . . The boat gave one spin round and slowly, ever so slowly, sunk beneath the waters. . . . her crew standing up, with hands outstretched, and faces such as I hope never to see more, till the waters rose over the last of them, drowning their dying cries."[21]

The Dog "Fraser"[22]

They said there was gold 'mid the
  Fraser's sands,
And it echoed o'er sea and shore,
Luring the stranger from distant lands,
Perchance to return no more.

And wild are the legends we often hear
And sorrowful of the tale:
"Here the men were drowned," and
  "over there
Is the spot where the Indian fell."

"And that dog that you see by the river
  bank,
Trudging wearily along its side,
Remembers the time when its master
  sank,
And his human comrade died.

"'Twas a dreary night and the howling
  wind
Sung the requiem of the dead;

And the voice of the drown'd man's
  canine friend
Hung over his watery bed.

"And every night, when the wind roars
  loud
He goes to the river's shore,
And gazes upon his master's shroud,
And cries as he did before.

Today he is seen where the waters rush
From the canyon's rude embrace;
And the miner's door he will freely push,
For his is a welcome face.

"But the morrow's sun will scarcely rise,
Ere the dog is far away.
But the one he seeks 'neath the waters
  lies,
Till the resurrection day."
      — HUDIBRAS

21. R. Byron Johnson, *Very Far West Indeed* (London: Marston, Low & Searle, 1872).

22. *British Columbian,* November 21, 1861.

The *British Columbian*'s editor commented that Hudibras was apparently unaware that "This poor and interesting dog died of a broken heart about two months ago near Lillooet" and suggested that Hudibras "might feel inclined to write his epithet." Shortly after, a response was published:

Epitaph on the Dog Fraser[23]

"*Hic Jacet*[24] — *Poor Fraser*"
Pause stranger here and mark this humble stone
Which simply tells one quality alone.
Seek not the record of the hero's fame,
The Patriot's virtue, or the Poet's name;
'Tis Fraser's grave, O, let your tribute be
One sorrowing thought for lost fidelity.

— NOT HUDIBRAS

Passengers who braved a paddlewheeler journey to Yale, the head of navigation, could expect to be ordered ashore to lighten the vessel as she struggled over a riffle, or be called upon to help "line" her through rapids as the frantic captain yelled for "More steam! More steam!" The vessels caught fire, ran into sandbars, ripped open on snags and rocks, or were blasted into splinters when their boiler exploded.

Five Jamieson brothers came to the Pacific Northwest from Scotland and found work on the steamers.[25] In 1854, one brother, whose name has been lost, perished when the *Gazelle* exploded in Oregon. In 1857, Robert Jamieson drowned when the *Portland* plunged over Oregon's Willamette Falls. In April, 1861 twenty-six year old Capt. Smith Jamieson lost his life when his *Fort Yale* exploded near Yale. In August, 1861 Capt. Archibald Jamieson

23. *British Columbian*, December 18, 1861.
24. "Hic Jacet" or "Hic Iacet" = "Here lies"

25. For more on the Jamiesons, see Roland Carey's "The Jamieson Brothers," *Pioneer Days in* *British Columbia*, Vol. 1. (Surrey: Foremost Publishing), 1973.

was piloting his sidewheeler *Cariboo* out of Victoria when her boiler erupted with a horrendous blast. This was a double tragedy for the bereaved Jamiesons in Scotland. Not only had they lost Archibald, but also the youngest brother, James, who had recently left Scotland to work with his brother.

On November 22, 1861, the paddlewheeler *Yale* foundered on a Fraser Canyon riffle and was swept into a whirlpool along with nineteen doomed men. "Hudibras" again picked up his pen.

In Memoriam[26]

Toll for the dead! brave hearts have perish'd,
From our firesides are the drown'd ones gone;
But in our memories they now are cherished,
Who yesterday were 'mong us every one.

Mourn for the dead! strong men have sunk
Beneath that river which retains its slain;
'Twas duty nerv'd them (cowards would have shrunk)
But duty's call they ne'er will heed again.

Weep for the dead! by home fires cheerful
Are those would weep but did they know
The news, which, making us so tearful,
Doth leave to them a heritage of woe.

Honor to the dead! In conq'ring nature
They conquer'd were. The victor stood
Alone. The world his wide theatre,
Lord of the mountain; monarch of the flood.

— HUDIBRAS

---

26. *British Columbian*, November 23, 1861.

In their quest for the mother lode prospectors struggled north to the Quesnel River, Keithley Creek, Antler, and over the mountain divide. Here, in early 1861 William "Dutch Bill" Dietz, one of a group camped beside a nameless brook which would become famous as Williams Creek, struck pay dirt. Vowing to keep their discovery secret, Dutch Bill and two associates returned to Antler for supplies. But Antler quickly divined that the trio were on to something big. Early next morning, when Dutch Bill quietly slipped out of town to returned to the strike, some citizens of Antler followed his snowshoe tracks and three hours after his return to Williams Creek the whole area had been staked.

The news spread like quicksilver. Miners labouring in the Fraser's sandbars packed up their gear and headed north, leaving hotelmen and entrepreneurs to face the boom's inevitable "bust." Hodge, whose Wayside House was situated five miles above Yale, stuck out the lean times for a while, then nailed a handwritten notice on his door:

My whisky's gone and credit, too
    And I've put out for Cariboo.
So if you want Rum, Gin or Ale
    You'll have to get it down in Yale.
        — "HODGE"[27]

Most roadhouses prided themselves on their hospitality and meals. A notable exception was one run by William "Scotty" Donaldson, a crusty Scotsman who was never without his tam-o'-shanter. His modest two-room establishment on the Bonaparte River was "filled with miners by day and night, sleeping under the table and benches as well as on top of them, and all over the floors."[28] When Walter Moberly stopped for a meal in 1862, Scotty "produced a frying pan full of stale flapjacks and a pan of milk. Each flapjack was about three inches in diameter and half an inch in thickness. Having demolished . . . the unsavory cakes . . . and drunk several cups of milk I asked Scotty what I had to pay, when he demanded fifty cents for each cake and fifty cents for each cup

27. *British Colonist*, July 29, 1863.

28. W. Champness. *To Cariboo and Back in 1862*

(Fairfield, WA: Ye Galleon Press, 1972).

British Columbia miners. BC ARCHIVES PDP-00014

of milk. This exorbitant charge so enraged my packer . . . that I had great difficulty in preventing a personal encounter."[29]

Scotty's hospitality turned from bad to worse, and the *Victoria Colonist* felt obliged to publish a warning:

> Look out for him. An old fellow known as Scotty keeps a hotel on the trail to Cariboo . . . and is the terror of travellers who go that way. He drinks hard and when in his cups an hallucination seizes him that he is about to be murdered and robbed and has been known to rise from his uneasy couch and, awakening his slumbering guests, driving them out of his house, leaving them there to shiver the remainder of the night in the open without blankets or the means of making a fire. Several travellers report having been used in this manner by Scotty, who is a clever sort of man when sober, but a demon when under the influence of drink.[30]

29. Walter Moberly. *The Rocks and Rivers of British Columbia* (London: H.

Blacklock, 1885).
30. See "Scotty Creek and Scottie Creek," in *Okanagan*

Historical Society of Vernon, BC Annual Report, 1941.

Cataline (Jean Caux) mule train loading for Babine Lake. BC ARCHIVES NO. A-03049

Pack trains laden with food, furniture, and mining equipment plodded along the hazardous trails to the mining camps. The most renowned packer was Jean Caux, who came from Catalonia on the border of France and Spain and thus became known as "Cataline."[31] Each of his four outfits had between 63 and 66 animals, five men, and a cook. The animals carried the same packs day after day and when the starting bell rang about 2 a.m. each would go to its own pack. The train was led by an experienced animal wearing a bell, the sound of which the others followed. They walked untied so that if one animal plunged off a cliff it would not pull the others after it.

Cataline, who had never gone to school, communicated in his unique language: a mixture of Chinook, French, English, Chinese, and Spanish. He kept all his records in his memory, which was remarkably accurate. As the narrow Cariboo trails were widened into wagon roads, Cataline took his mules and horses into more remote, roadless areas. He packed in the Omineca and

31. Many articles have been written about Cataline. See, for example, Garnet Basque's "Jean Caux, the Man They Called 'Cataline'" in *Frontier Days in British Columbia* (Langley: Sunfire Publications, 1993).

in 1898 packed from Telegraph Creek to Atlin for the Yukon Field Force. His last home was Hazelton, where he died in 1922.

Mike Tuohy (1872–1949) homesteaded just south of Francois Lake in 1909. He was a well-known character and is credited with introducing the first threshing machine into the area in 1920. (Until then threshing had been done with a flail or with horses tramping out the grain.) He was the Lake District's tall tale champion until he met Joe Lougheed. Mike recalled, "Joe stayed with me and lied far into the night. In the morning I primed him with a cup of coffee and he lied until noon." Mike's verses record his observations of the land and the people around him, including this poem about Cataline.

Graham and Cataline[32]

From the far off Walla Walla
To the shores of Lake Babine
Was the trail they used to travel
Rain-washed now and seldom seen.

Through the Flathead Reservation
And across the boundary line
Winds the trail they used to travel,
Graham[33] and Cataline.

Where the totem poles were mileposts
And the Indian Rancheree
Was the source of trade and commerce
That was north of fifty-three.

Where the boundless wealth is waiting
In the forests and the mines
And the men that blazed a pathway
Were Graham and Cataline.

Now in Hazelton they're sleeping
Those old timers side by side
And they're throwing diamond hitches
Far across the great Divide.

Then we'll meet them from the forest
From the farms and from the mines
From the land of diamond hitches
We'll meet Graham and Cataline.

And they'll tell us of that country
That country strange and new
When the trails they were unknown
And there were only just a few

Just a few that know the wilderness,
The women and the wine
Like that glorious Jack Graham
And that peerless Cataline.

— MIKE TUOHY

---

32. Pat Turkki. *Burns Lake and District* (Burns Lake:

Burns Lake Historical Society, 1973).

33. Jack Graham has unfortunately faded from memory.

In July, 1858, Governor Douglas promised that "as soon as good and trusted men are found" the government would, for a small fee, provide an escort to ensure safe delivery of gold from the mines to the Treasury. The plan was not put into effect until 1861, when ten men, supplied with arms and horses, provided an inaugural escort from Port Douglas on Harrison Lake. However, as the government neither guaranteed safe delivery of the gold nor accepted responsibility for its loss, miners and bankers spurned the service, the public ridiculed it, and the *British Columbian* joined in the derision. The following lines were written upon the death of Capt. Nind's steed, which "shuffled off its mortal coil" near the New Westminster cricket grounds.

Captain Nind's Steed[34]

Come drop a tear, for this poor horse
Had once a decent name
But alas! he joined the Escort,
And died of grief and shame.

And now no more he'll follow
The cart along the track

Nor clamber over mountains
With a "Greeny" on his back.

Then may the "gray backs" ne'er disturb
His bones — where they now rest
For well they know that while he lived
He always did his best.

— ANONYMOUS

The escort was disbanded until 1863, when a triple murder and robbery at Quesnel Forks spurred its revival — again with no guarantee of delivery. Stories were told of lost receipts and disclosures of confidential figures. "We cannot easily forget the miserable bungling attempt made nearly two years ago — a display of stupid incapacity we hope never to see repeated."[35] When the corps showed expenditures of $60,000 against an income of $6,000, it was disbanded for good.

---

34. *British Columbian,*
August 12, 1862.

35. *British Columbian,*
March 7, 1863.

One of the hopefuls who joined the rush to Cariboo was John A. Fraser, son of explorer Simon Fraser. On Simon's death in 1862, the impoverished family mortgaged its farm and property in St. Andrews, Ontario and used the proceeds to send John to the Cariboo to invest in promising mines. John became a prominent Barkerville citizen. He was a member of the Masonic Lodge, a strong voice in the Methodist choir, President of the Literary Society and the Library Association. When gold was found on the Prince of Wales claim, in which he had an interest, he was jubilant.

The Miner to His Claim [36]

Good morning, noble "Prince of Wales" the sun is shining bright,
And, like the lovely morn, you fill my bosom with delight;
Thy "washing up" each morning fills with gladness every eye,
Then who would not, most noble Prince, extol thee to the sky?

Chorus:
Drift away! hoist away, pound away the earth,
Rattle up the dump box, to bring the treasure forth;
And whether 'tis in "fine dust," in "nuggets," or in "scales"
We thank thee for thy pleasant gifts, most "noble Prince of Wales."

I know thou art my dearest friend, both generous and free,
And all my feelings flow, dear Prince, in gratitude to thee;
Before a "prospect" proved thy worth, on thee I "went my pile,"
And now, each morn, I dearly love to see thy golden smile.

'Tis said that man was made of dust when first the world began.
And even in these later days 'tis "dust" that makes the man;
A fact you know full well, dear Prince, so let the neighbours see
A veritable man of dust in each that sticks to thee.

---

36. E/B/F 865.9. BC Archives.

There's Camp a social, generous soul, and loyal to the core,
Bilsland, Dinwoodin, and of Johns a round half dozen more;
When far from thee and Cariboo they'll spin their mining tales
And toast thy splendor o'er and o'er, thou glorious "Prince of Wales."

And Prince, through all vicissitudes of sunshine and of shade,
I'll stick to thee though friends around loud murmurings have made;
And when thy golden reign is o'er, to Mary I will flee,
And that's a lovely reason, Prince, why you should stick to me.

And Prince, there is another prince, far o'er the rolling sea;
Among the Princes of the earth, there's none like him and thee;
And both are made of sterling stuff, of nature's virgin mould,
He is the Prince of Britain's Isle, and thou the Prince of Gold.

Oh! Prince, thy sympathetic heart to death would surely bleed,
For thousands here, in Cariboo, who cannot find the "lead";
But still, for all the miseries a miner's life entails,
May each yet find in Cariboo a special "Prince of Wales."

    — JOHN A. FRASER

John Fraser passed the winter of 1863–64 in Victoria, where he was successful in becoming a BC surveyor. He placed an ad in the April 2nd, 1864 *British Columbian* under "John A. Fraser, Mining Engineer and Surveyor, Cameronton, BC", and stated that he had "recently provided himself with a complete set of instruments of unsurpassed excellence."

His return to Barkerville was dogged by misfortune and/or mismanagement. He neglected to keep up the mortgage payments on the family farm and was faced with the prospect of defending himself in a pending lawsuit. On May 18, his mind was "slightly wandering" and towards evening, "the symptoms assumed a more alarming form, rendering the patient very violent." On the 19th, he showed considerable improvement but the following day he received two letters: one advising that the mortgage had been foreclosed, the other that his fiancée had married. John "put an end to his existence with a small pen knife. . . . His remains were borne to their last resting place by his Masonic brethren and by the largest concourse of friends ever before assembled in Cariboo for such a purpose. . . . He has found a grave in the land which his father gave to the world."[37]

"The Broken Miner" seems to have been John's last poem.

The Broken Miner[38]

Last night as in sweet sleep I lay,
My dreaming thoughts roamed far away,
The scenes my early childhood knew
In smiling freshness rose to view;

Then passed before me pure and mild
A mother, bending o'er her child,
Again those clarion accents rung
"O leave us not, my darling son."

Chorus:
Then let our chorus loudly ring,
The Broken Miner's lot I sing,
Most bitter is the lot indeed
Of him who cannot find the "lead."

The midnight hours roll slowly past,
And coldly blows the northern blast,
No more, to-night, will tranquil sleep
In sweet repose my spirit keep.

My blankets thin, and cabin cold,
Proclaim how vain this thirst for gold!
Most wretched is the lot indeed
Of him who cannot find the "lead."

— JOHN A. FRASER

37. *British Columbian*, June 1, 1865.

38. *Cariboo Sentinel*, October 29, 1866.

James Anderson (1839–1923) left Scotland in 1863 to make his fortune in the Cariboo. He was a popular figure in Barkerville, where his poems enlivened social gatherings as well as the pages of the *Cariboo Sentinel*. Many of Anderson's poems were purported to be letters to Sawney, a friend in Scotland. His most popular poem celebrates the arrival of Madame Bendikson and her troupe of "hurdy-gurdy" dancing girls. Their advent called for a little sprucing up. One entrepreneur advertised that, "In consequence of the great influx of the Fair Sex," he was "prepared to give his Patrons HOT and COLD BATHS in the best style." Not to be outdone, a rival "fitted up a BATHROOM at considerable expense" and also offered to "attend to Extracting, Filling and Cleaning of Teeth."[39]

The German Lasses[40]

Last summer we had lassies here
Frae Germany — the hurdies, O!
And troth I wot, as I'm a Scot
They were the bonnie hurdies, O!

There was Kate and Mary, blithe and
   airy,
And dumpy little Lizzy, O!
An' ane they ca'd the kangaroo,
A trappin', rattlin' hizzy, O!

They danced at nicht in dresses light,
Frae late until the early, O!
But oh! their hearts were hard as flint,
Which vexed the laddies sairly, O!

The dollar was their only love,
And that they loved fu' dearly, O!
They dinna care a flea for men,
Let them coort hooe'r sincerely, O!

They left the creek wi' lots o' gold,
Danced frae oor lads sae clever, O!
My blessin's on their "sour kraut" heads,
Gif they stay awa for ever, O!

Chorus:
Bonnie are the hurdies, O!
The German hurdy-gurdies, O!
The daftest hour that e'r I spent
Was dancin' wi' the hurdies, O!

— JAMES ANDERSON

39. *Cariboo Sentinel*, July 20 and September 6, 1866.
40. James Anderson. *Sawney's Letters and Cariboo Rhymes*. Barkerville Restoration Advisory Committee of the Province of British Columbia (Victoria: Queen's Printer, 1962).

The Hurdies. German dancing girls at Barkerville. BC ARCHIVES G-00817

Frontiersmen often became attached to the rough log cabins that provided shelter and comfort, however minimal. Those with poetic leanings wrote tributes to their humble dwellings, as did James Anderson.

The Prospector's Shanty [41]

See yonder shanty on the hill,
'Tis but an humble biggin'
Some ten by six within the wa's
Your head may touch the riggin'

The door stands open to the south,
The fire, outside the door;
The logs are chinket close wi' fog
And nocht but mud the floor

41. Ibid.

A knife an' fork, a pewter plate,
An' cup o' the same metal,
A teaspoon an' a sugar bowl,
A frying pan an' kettle;

The bakin' board hangs on the wa',
Its purposes are twa-fold —
For mixing bread wi' yeast or dough
Or panning oot the braw gold!

A log or twa in place o' stools,
A bed withoot a hangin',
Are feckly a' the furnishin's
This little house belangin';

The laird and tennant o' this sty,
I canna name it finer,
Lives free an' easy as a lord,
Tho' but an "honest miner."

— JAMES ANDERSON

Francis J. Barnard arrived in Yale in 1859. He was purser on the Fort Yale when it exploded and was one of the few survivors.[42] Turning to a less hazardous occupation he became an express-man in competition with "Billy" Ballou. The two rivals scrambled over the footpaths between Yale and the Cariboo — 610 km each way — packing letters and newspapers on their backs. For every letter delivered they collected $2. Newspapers sold for $1 each.[43] By 1862, Barnard had done so well he was able to buy horses and inaugurate his pony express; the horses carried the mail while Barnard walked. When the wagon road to Cariboo was completed Barnard's Express ("the B.X.") was ready with sturdy stage coaches, expert drivers and some 30 horses.

James Anderson laboured in the Cariboo for eight years but "fortune, we are sorry to say, has not smiled on him; and weary of wooing her embraces in the search for gold, he now returns to his old Scottish home, where a fond wife and family have long been mourning his absence."[44] He returned to Scotland and later moved to England where he died in 1923. Anderson, who no doubt spent anxious hours waiting for Barnard's Express to bring word from home, penned the following:

42. See "In Memoriam," p. 33.

43. E.O.S. Scholefield, "The Yale-Cariboo Wagon Road, Part One," *The British Columbia Magazine*, February, 1911, p. 93. See also Pat Foster's "The B.C. Express Company . . ." in *British Columbia Historical News*, Summer, 1998.

44. *Cariboo Sentinel*, June 25, 1868.

Waiting for the Mail[45]

Man's life is like a medley
Composed of many airs,
Which makes us glad or make us sad,
And oft our laughter dares;
E'en so our hearts have many cords
And strains of light and strong,
Which makes us glad or makes us sad,
Like changes in the song;
Our smiles and tears, our hopes and fears,
Our sorrows never fail —
But ev'ry heart knows not the smart
Of waiting for the mail.

A teamster from the Beaver Pass —
"What news of the Express?"
"'Twas there last night, if I heard right;
'Twill be in to-day I guess."
A miner next, on Williams Creek
Arrived from wint'ring south,
He heard some say 'twould be to-day
Expected at the Mouth.[46]
But here comes Poole, in haste his
    rule —
"Hallo! what of the mail?"
From him we learn, with some concern,
"Just two days out from Yale!"

Ah! waiting is a weariness,
"The Express is at Van Winkle!"
This makes the face deny the case,
And quite removes a wrinkle.
A few hours more — a great uproar —
The express is come at last!
An Eastern mail, see by the bale,

As "Sullivan" goes past;
An' now an eager, anxious crowd
Awaits the letter sale,
Postmaster curst — their "wrath was nurs'd"
By waiting for the mail.

"Hurrah!" at length the window's up —
"There's nothing, John, for me?"
John knows the face — the letter place —
"Two bits on that," says he.
And many come and many go
In sorrow or delight
While some will say their's "met delay,"
Whose friend forgot to write;
An anxious heart who stands apart
Expectant of a letter,
With hopeful mind but fears to find
Some loved one still his debtor.

The day is passed, the office closed.
The letters are deliver'd
And some have joy without alloy
While some fond hopes are shiver'd;
The sweetheart wed — a dear friend
    dead,
Or closer tie is broken.
Ah! many an ache the heart may take
By words tho' never spoken.
But whether good or bad the news
This happens without fail,
Your letter read-the fire is fed
For waiting on the Mail.
                    — JAMES ANDERSON

---

45. James Anderson,
Sawney's Letters. Op. cit.

46. Quesnellemouth is
today's Quesnel.

The proposed Collins Overland Telegraph was to link North America with Europe via San Francisco, New Westminster, northern BC and Alaska. An underwater cable would cross the Bering Sea, stretch to Siberia, and connect with the Russian telegraph. US Col. Charles Bulkley, after whom the Bulkley River was named, was engineer-in-chief of the project. Excitement rippled through the Cariboo in September 1865 when the telegraph reached Quesnel. In 1866, as the line approached the upper Nass River and surveyors were slashing a route past Telegraph Creek, a message flashed through the wires to Quesnel — an undersea cable linking the two continents had been laid across the Atlantic. Although the Collins project was abandoned, a line remained in use as far as Quesnel and was extended to Barkerville in 1868. Tal O. Eifon, whose poems often appeared in the *Cariboo Sentinel*, mused over the implications.

Lines to the Telegraph[47]

Who can tell what wire's worth
When it's wound around the earth,
Bearing safe o'er land and sea
Flashing electricity?
Telegraph with mystic hands
Reveals the news of many lands;
Honest, faithful, silent slave,
Serving both the just and knave.
There's nothing like the Telewag,
Altho' the bulky letterbag
We must confess was quite a boon
When it arrived but once a moon!
In those days when news came slow,
Often stopped by rain or snow,
How we used to guess and guess

What news we'd have by next Express!
Now we'll know per Operator
Those news ahead and something later.
Soon we'll know in Cariboo
The doings of the dark Hindoo,
And we'll hear within a day
What the folks in Europe say; . . .

All their talk will in a twinkle
Be rushing madly past Van Winkle,
Quicker than the rushing wind,
Leaving everything else behind,
Coming from an Eastern clime,
Chasing, racing, beating Time.
             — TAL O. EIFON

47. *Cariboo Sentinel*, July 9, 1868.

Barkerville's Black community included Rebecca Gibbs, a pious lady whose poems were published in the *Cariboo Sentinel*.[48] A native of Philadelphia, she joined the rush to Cariboo and by 1868 had established a laundry in Barkerville. She later moved to Victoria where she died in 1873 at the age of 60. This poem is carved on her tombstone in Ross Bay Cemetery.

The Old Red Shirt[49]

A miner came to my cabin door,
His clothes they were covered with dirt;
He held out a piece he desired me to
    wash,
Which I found was an old red shirt.

His cheeks were thin, and furrow'd his
    brow,
His eyes they were sunk in his head;
He said that he had got work to do,
[To] be able to earn his bread.

He said that the "old red shirt" was
    torn,
And asked me to give it a stitch;
But it was threadbare, and sorely worn,
Which show'd he was far from rich.

Of miners with good paying claims,
O! traders who wish to do good,
Have pity on men who earn your
    wealth,
Grudge not the poor miner his food.

Far from these mountains a poor
    mother mourns
The darling that hung by her skirt,
When contentment and plenty sur-
    rounded the home
Of the miner that brought me the shirt.
                    — REBECCA GIBBS

---

48. For an account of black pioneers in British Columbia, see Crawford Kilian's *Go Do Some Great Thing* (Vancouver: Douglas and McIntyre, 1978).

49. James Anderson. *Sawney's Letters*, op. cit.

In 1864 Barnard's Express inaugurated a weekly passenger service from Clinton to Lillooet, a distance of some 76 km. Passengers were often pressed into service to help push wagons up hills, repair broken parts, clear snow slides, and extricate mired coaches. Slides and washouts were frequent hazards. One traveler reported, "In places the hillside is almost precipitous, and on rounding a sharp bend one offers up a silent prayer that the stage may not overturn and land us in the river five hundred feet below, for the driver takes a fiendish delight in dashing along at breakneck speed, much to the discomfiture of the poor passenger."[50] Passengers were often in a state of terror. "The driver, who was intoxicated, commenced whipping his horses furiously, and kept them at full gallop for about two miles, when one of the wheels struck a stone, causing the tongue to break in two. . . . [the horses became] completely ungovernable, and they dashed on at full speed, the wagon swaying from side to side, and bouncing over the stony road in the most alarming manner."[51] Miraculously, no lives were lost on this route.

"On the Lillooet Road" has been attributed to Arthur Martley, son of Capt. John Martley.[52] Arthur was a teamster, prospector, trapper, and farmer in the Lillooet District, but his biggest adventure occurred after he had retired and unexpectedly fell heir to a $125,000 fortune left to him by a cousin in India. Arthur immediately married a woman some 44 years his junior, and embarked on a honeymoon voyage to India to collect his inheritance. The couple continued to Europe but, "according to Mr. Martley, their matrimonial barque was wrecked in Rome . . . [where] he lost his bride . . . and only recovered her, after diligent search, in London."[53] His bride estranged, and a goodly portion of his inheritance unaccountably missing, Arthur returned to BC. He fell in with three American aviators and with them flew to Mexico to throw in his lot with the revolutionaries. Mexican authorities

50. C. F. J. Galloway. *The Call of the West* (London: Unwin, 1916).
51. *British Columbian*, August, 1865. Quoted in

"The Yale-Cariboo Wagon-Road, Part Two." E. O. S. Scholefield, in *Man-to-Man Magazine*, January–February 1911.

52. See "Mr. Doolan's Lament," p. 66.
53. "Lillooet Man's Shattered Romance," in the *Daily Province*, May 2, 1924.

Near the Bridge on the Lillooet Road BC ARCHIVES I-33341

promptly arrested him and jailed him in Vera Cruz. On his
release, he worked his way back to Vancouver on a tramp steamer.
He died in Lillooet in 1942 at the age of 87.

On the Lillooet Road[54]

Driving on the Lillooet road
Through rain and snow and cold,
With a resolution bold,
Driving on the Lillooet road.
Four men with whip and line
Keep up with flying time,
Driving on the Lillooet road;
Hear those teamsters singing?
Each one has his mode.
Hear those sleigh bells ringing?
Driving on the Lillooet road.

Bill Keathly with the whip
Cuts his horses on the hip;
Driving on the Lillooet road.
He makes a trip a week,
While his horses sweat and reek,
Driving on the Lillooet road.
See those hills before you?
They're terrors with a load;
Let whip and lines adorn you.
Driving on the Lillooet road. . . .

Arthur Martley's eyes are bright,
For he travels in the night,
Driving on the Lillooet road.
He's as slow as a crawling snail —
To reach home he'll often fail,

Driving on the Lillooet road.
See those bluffs above you?
Birds of prey's abode —
The scenery would move you,
Driving on the Lillooet road.

Bob Cummings drives with two,
For he's nothing much to do,
Driving on the Lillooet road.
His horses they are fat
When they ain't poor's a bat,
Driving on the Lillooet road.
See that stream below you?
For ages it has flowed.
The Fraser River, know you?
Driving on the Lillooet road.

There's Fred, who drives the stage,
Small, but yet of age,
Driving on the Lillooet road.
He goes there in a day,
Stays a night, and then away,
Driving on the Lillooet road.
Hear those wheels a-rattling
Beneath their heavy load?
Hear those whips a-crackling?
Driving on the Lillooet Road.
                        — ARTHUR MARTLEY [?]

54. Arthur Martley [?]. *Bridge River-Lillooet News*, May 3, 1934. J. N. J. Brown fonds. North Vancouver Museum and Archives.

In 1868, the B.X. bought some 400 horses in California and Mexico and drove them north to present-day Vernon — the start of the B.X. horse ranch. The B.X. never bought a "broke" horse, which was regarded as spoiled. Veteran driver Willis West recalled that with proper training the wild horses developed "into beautiful animals which the hostellers were more than proud to lead out for the admiration of the stage passengers. . . . It was remarkable how rapidly they learned what was expected of them . . . the horses seemed as concerned as the driver in ensuring that the stage arrived safely." The best-known "whip" was Steve Tingley, who "handled the ribbons" for the B.X. for 28 years. Of the drivers' skill, West said, "If you had been a passenger on top of a heavily loaded six-horse stage in the spring and had watched the driver take the stage down an icy mountain hill you would almost certainly have a more concrete appreciation of the skill and courage required by a driver"[55] The drivers made it a point to enter and leave all stations in a galloping flourish, with none more proud of this than the horses themselves.

There were accidents. "Near 64-Mile House, an avalanche gave way under the stage, "precipitating passengers, horses and wagon over the bank, falling and rolling about 150 feet. One passenger suffered a broken leg, split kneecap, and hip injuries; another escaped with a sprained ankle. Both lead horses died immediately. Driver Alex Tingley, though badly bruised, ran five km to Nicomen for help. He arrived 'minus coat and boots' but secured prompt assistance." [56]

On another occasion when a coach upset, "a passenger, Mrs. F. W. Foster, was thrown clear over the edge of the road to light in a treetop near . . . Spuzzum, while the agile [driver], landing on his feet, sprang upon the axle of the two front wheels and rode there until he brought the frightened horses to a stop.[57]

---

55. Willis J. West, "Staging in the Cariboo," *B.C. Historical Quarterly*, July, 1948.
56. E. O. S. Scholefield,

"The Yale–Cariboo Wagon-Road," in *Man-to-Man Magazine*, January, 1911.
57. "Feats of Noted Stage

Driver," *The Province*, February 1, 1936.

The Wraith of the Trail[58]

There's a grass grown trail near the shining rail where the trains goes whizzing by —
Where the smoke from the overland fast express is spread like a veil in the sky;
It's the trail where the stage went rumbling through in the days of the real frontier,
But where is the driver who braved the path and whose stout heart knew no fear?

'Twas a perilous trip that the prairie ship made across the high, brown plains,
But has any one ever heard men tell of a coward who held the reins?
There are plenty of tales of heroes' work and of passengers saved from death,
But when did a driver ever quail in the fiercest blizzard's breath?

So go to the trail when the stars are pale and 'tis scarce an hour till dawn,
And you'll see a ghostly stage flit past, by four ghost horses drawn;
And high on the box sits the ghost of a man, and he throws you an eerie hail —
It is thus that the stage goes by today on the grass-grown overland trail.

    — ARTHUR CHAPMAN

While gold fever raged along the Fraser, numerous prospectors were slipping across BC's southern interior border, thus avoiding the required customs and license fees. Governor James Douglas countered this breach by sending customs officers to places such as Similkameen, Rock Creek and Osoyoos. From their reports we learn of the earliest settlers in these areas, one of whom was Harry Wend.

Wend had kept a tavern at Hope but in 1862 was lured to Cherry Creek by a gold discovery there. He is credited with building the first house — a log cabin — in the White Valley (Lumby area). It was to be "a house of entertainment." Leonard Norris (1862–1945), poet and founder of the Vernon-based Okanagan Historical Society, paid tribute to Wend's enterprise.

58. Arthur Chapman. *West-ward Ho!* (Vancouver: British Columbia Magazine Co., n.d.), p. 363.

The House of Wend[59]

— a Lumby Legend

Where blooms the thorn and the wild
   thyme
And Whitevale's wooded slopes incline
Mid hazel brush and tangled vine,
A house was built with logs of pine
Near by the river's bend,
With but one window and one door
And sixteen feet by twenty-four
This rude log house the legend bore
"The House of Wend."

A wayside inn wherein might rest
The mining man by pack opprest,
And find himself an honoured guest
With fare and liquors of the best,
And wines of finest blend;
And sit at ease while tales went round
Of placer diggings newly found
With gold galore in shallow ground
In House of Wend.

But no guest entered at the door
And no guest trod the dried-mud floor
And no one stood his bar before
And all the mining men forebore
Their hard-earned cash to spend;
Till when the season's work was o'er
On Cherry Creek about two score
Of mining men appeared before
The House of Wend.

They said: "Those diggings have us
   beat.

We struggled hard against defeat,
For weeks we lived on gophers meat
Till hunger forced us to retreat
Without a dividend."
They camped beneath the trees, and
   then
They lit their fires, these bearded men,
For that was good enough for them,
They said to Wend.

To Wend it was a doleful sight
Their camp fires burning in the night
Shedding abroad their warmth and
   light,
And all his future prospects bright
Of business at an end;
And hot resentment flushed his face
That one and all should shun his place,
"To find some guests my board to grace
I go," said Wend.

Then brooding still and ill content
Straightway he rolled his pack and
   went
On finding paying guests intent —
Free spenders all; and backward sent
No word to foe or friend.
But from that day the owl or bat
Or skunk or squirrel or bush-tailed rat,
Were all that ever entered at
The door of Wend.
On far-off trails from day to day
A lone man sullen, bent, and grey
A solitary waif and stray

---

59. *The Okanagan Historical Society of Vernon, BC Annual Report,* 1939.

For ever onward, took his way,
    Praying his luck would mend.
With beard descending on his breast
He still pursued his weary quest,
Still looking for a paying guest
    Went Harry Wend.

Now where the ancient ruin sits,
At midnight oft a spectre skips,
And lifts a bottle to its lips,
    Winks and beckons to men, then slips
Smirking around the bend;
And the settlers shiver with fear,
When they see the phantom appear,
Run and yell and ne'er go near
    The House of Wend.

— LEONARD NORRIS

Stagecoach on Cariboo Road BC ARCHIVES A-09775

Great plans were constantly afoot for building roads and railways into BC's hinterlands in order to tap the province's abundant resources. Surveyors struggled through canyons and mountain passes in search of practicable routes. J. H. Secretan (1852–1926) joined the CPR in 1871 as assistant engineer and helped survey the railway line across Canada. After a sojourn in the Cariboo, he was assigned, in 1875, to the head of Bute Inlet with orders to run a line up the Homathko River. He recorded that, "These Homathco Canyons were very difficult to negotiate and many a time I was slung up with a line under my armpits laboriously trying to find room for the tripod of a transit on a narrow ledge of projecting rock, often many hundred feet above the foaming whirling white waters of the stream below. I spent two years on this route."[60]

In later years, he surveyed in Saskatchewan, where he discovered the bodies of several Cree recently murdered and scalped by an enemy tribe. He took "a particularly perfect" skull and had the camp's cook clean and sandpaper it. Skull in hand, he mused over his career, picked up his pencil, and wrote on the dome:

Long have I roamed these dreary
   plains,
I've used up horses, men and brains;
And, oft from virtue's path I've strayed
To find a fifty-two-foot grade.
But now, thank God, I'll take a rest,

Content, I've done my level best;
To this green Earth I'll say farewell
And run a Railway line through Hell.
   — J. H. SECRETAN

J. N. J. Brown's Native mother gave birth to him under a pine tree near Lillooet while she was accompanying her prospector husband to their homestead in the Empire Valley. In spite of Brown's sketchy education — the nearest school was about 140 km distant

60. J.H. Secretan. *Canada's Great Highway* (London: John Lane, 1924). Secretan also authored *Out West* and *To Klondyke and Back*. (London: Hurst and Blackett, 1898).

— he developed a love for language and poetry. In 1885, from his home at Empire Ranch, BC, he published *The Rural Backwoodsman*, the first newspaper in the Lillooet district. He was an ardent sculler and won BC's single scull championship in 1908. But his heart was in the hills, where he had several mining interests and where he no doubt blazed many trails. He published numerous historical articles plus two collections of verse, *Western Fragments* and *Prospector's Trail*. He died in Vancouver in 1942.

"The Pathfinder's" sentiments might well be echoed by many whose names are forgotten: James McDougall, who scouted the way for Simon Fraser's entry into New Caledonia; Jacco Finlay, who cleared a trail over the Rockies for David Thompson; and the people of the First Nations, over whose tracks most of BC's lines of communication were built.

The Pathfinder[61]

Long years ago I blazed a trail
Through lovely woods unknown till
    then,
And marked with cairns of splintered
    shale
A mountain way for other men.

For other men who came and came;
They trod the path more plain to see,
They gave my trail another's name
And no one speaks or knows of me.

The trail runs high, the trail runs low,
Where wild flowers dance, or
    columbine;
The scars are healed that long ago
My axe cut deep on birch and pine.

Another's name my trail may bear,
But still I keep, in waste and wood,
My joy because the trail is there,
My peace because the trail is good.
                        — J. N. J. BROWN

61. North Vancouver Museum and Archives have scrapbooks containing clipping of Brown's published articles as well as his poems.

The call of unexplored wilderness lured many pioneers into the "beyond." R. Alpine McGregor, born circa 1855 in the Orkney Islands, came to Canada while in his twenties and prospected — unsuccessfully — in Northern Ontario. He served in WWI, was wounded, and recuperated in England. He returned to Canada with a wife and settled — for a while — on Cortes Island. He prospected BC's coastline by gas boat and wrote extensively. In 1925, "The Call" overtook him and he joined the "Red Lake Stampede" in Northern Ontario.

The Call[62]

Let me start now! forever let me go!
An old tump-line, a pick, tobacco, roll.
An axe, snare-wire, some matches and
  a pipe;
A book of simple verse to tune my soul
To those gay winds which northward
  blow
On wings of mallard, geese and snipe.

Spread out a northern map! The
  unexplored
of rivers, lakes and forests wide;
A tent, canoe, a lard pail and a knife;
And let my truant heart be guide —
Prithee, my master, 'pon my word
'Tis for the north I'd leave my life.
                    — R. ALPINE MCGREGOR

George Mercer Dawson's (1849–1901) childhood was marred when he developed tuberculosis of the spine. The disease caused his back to twist and curve, leaving him with stunted growth and a large humpback. He studied geology and in 1873 joined the North American Boundary Commission as geologist and botanist. In 1875, he was appointed to the Geological Survey of Canada. In spite of his severe deformity he covered an astounding amount of rugged territory in BC and the Yukon (Dawson

62. E. L. Chicanot, ed., *Rhymes of the Miner: An*   *Anthology of Canadian Mining Verse* (Gardenvale,   Quebec: Federal Publications Limited, 1937).

Miner, Rocky Mountains, 1864. BC ARCHIVES PDP-00028

City is named for him), mapping and collecting botanical and geological specimens. He studied the languages and customs of the First Nations people and collected artifacts. He wrote numerous reports on the province's geology and natural resources. He sometimes jotted drafts of verse in his daily journal or on scraps of paper — verse he did not intend to publish.

In Keremeos, he puzzled over the occurrence of green rocks which " have slipped in again without proving their connexion with the quartzites properly, or their right to appear at all." His perplexity flowed into verse.[63]

Oh! for a fossil, Some poor shell
That died upon that olden shore
But yet in whispered voice can tell,
Last hollow throbbing of a bell —
Of the old ocean's roar.

At Cluculz Creek (near Vanderhoof) he noticed a delicate flower:

Just as a wee maid when she stands
with downcast eyes and folded hands
to say her oft conn'd task
So blushing on some mossy bank
where days are long and woods are
   dank,
or crowded thick twixt lichened stones

where some old glacier laid his bones;
Those nodding bells are swung.
Fairer than all, where all are fair
within the flowery band,
and breathing out a perfume rare
where the tall ranked pine trees stand
in the lone distant northern land.

Thoughts of the eternal were engendered on the Pacific's shores:

To rest on fragrant cedar boughs
Close by the western ocean's rim,
While in the tops of giant pines
The live-long night the sea-winds
   hymn,

And low upon the fretted shore
The waves beat out the evermore.[64]

63. Douglas Cole and Bradley Lockner, eds. *The Journals of George M. Dawson: British Columbia, 1875-1878. V. II,* (Vancouver: UBC Press, 1989).

64. *Transactions of the Royal Society of Canada,* Section IV, 1902, p. 183.

Preparing for a grueling journey into the BC wilderness, he speculated that:

Contorted beds, of unknown age,
My weary limbs shall bear,
Perhaps a neat synclinal fold
At night shall be my lair.
Dips I shall take on unnamed streams,
Or where the rocks strike, follow
Along the crested mountain ridge

Or anticlinal hollow;
Or gently with the hammer stroke
The slumbering petrifaction,
That for a hundred million years
Has been debarred from action.[65]
— GEORGE MERCER DAWSON

Dawson's stamina, determination and willingness to share camp work, won him the respect of all he came in contact with. At night, around the campfires, everyone enjoyed hearing him recount his adventures. British-born Clive Phillipps-Wolley (1854–1918) arrived in BC circa 1896. He was an ardent sportsman and adventurer who wrote extensively. When he heard that "The Little Doctor" had died in Ottawa, he composed a tribute to his friend.[66]

To Dr. George[67]

High above us, on Mount Sicker, I can
  hear the blue grouse hoot,
Birds are calling, rivers glitter, buds are
  bursting, grasses shoot;
On the pine stump, by our shanty,
  Dawson's tattered map lies spread,
And my partner with his finger marks
  the footsteps of the dead. . . .

Hope she has fooled us often
but we follow her spring call yet,
And we'd risk our lives on *his* say so

and steer the course he set;
Down the Dease and the lonely Liard
from Yukon to Stickine,
There's always a point to swear by,
where the little doctor's been,
Who made no show of his learning,
but, Lord! what he didn't know
Hadn't the worth of country rock,
the substance of summer snow.
I guess had he chosen, maybe,
he'd have quit the noise and fuss
of cities and high palavers,

65. Ibid., p. 185.
66. For an account of Wolley's activities in BC see Murray, Peter. *Home from the*

Hill: Three Gentlemen Adventurers (Victoria: Horsdal & Schubert, 1994).
67. Clive Phillipps-Wolley.

Songs of an English Esau (London: Smith, Elder, 1902).

to throw in his lot with us.
He'd crept so close to nature
he could hear what the Big Things say,
Our Arctic nights and our Northern
   lights,
our winds and pines at play.
He loved his work and his workmates
and all as he took for wage
Was the name his brave feet traced him
on Northland's newest page.

That and the hearts of the hard-fists
though I reckon for work well done —

He who set the stars for guide lights
will keep him the place he won;
Will lead him safe through the passes
and over the Last Divide
To the Camp of Honest Workers
of men who never lied,
And tell him the boys he worked for, say
judging as best they can,
That in lands that try manhood hardest,
he was tested and proved a man.

— CLIVE PHILLIPPS-WOLLEY

George Winkler, known as "the prospector poet," came to BC from Ontario in 1897. He was in Victoria in 1908, and resided at times in Penticton, the Queen Charlottes, and Princeton. His prospecting eventually led him to a rich copper ore deposit at Jordan River. He died in Saanich in 1978 at the age of 104, leaving to BC Archives some 500 photos he had taken on his many BC journeys.

"Father Pat" was Irish-born Rev. Henry Irwin (1859–1901), an Anglican who was devoted to "his" miners and moved easily amongst them. Of all the clergymen who served in BC's pioneer days, Father Pat was undoubtedly the most compassionate and beloved, as evident in Winkler's poems.[68]

---

68. For more on Father Pat see Elsie G. Turnbull's "Mileposts of History along Highway 3" in *Pioneer Days in British Columbia*, Vol. 4 (Surrey: Heritage House, 1979), and George Fraser's "Father Pat" in *The Okanagan Historical Society of Vernon, BC Annual Report*, 1950.

Henry (Father Pat) Irwin
BC ARCHIVES B-09815

Father Pat[69]

We don't go much on parsons,
Here in the minin' belt
'Tween Rossland and the Similkameen;
But there was one we felt
A most uncommon likin' for —
You take my word for that; —
The latch-string hung outside each door
For good friend Father Pat.

He wore the Church of England brand,
But didn't bank on creeds;
His way to hearts was not with words,
But helpful, lovin' deeds.
Though we were hard to work upon,
Not readily enticed —
We called him *the* first Christian
That ever lived — since Christ.

He never peeked at keyholes,
Nor fought the cigarette;
He never frowned on lager beer,
Nor games of chance, — and yet,
I think that if there is a place
Where good souls get their dues,
They'll find room there for Father Pat
'Fore preachers you might choose

He never built no churches,
Nor learned to primp or pose;
His shoes were red and dusty,
And he *never* wore good clothes.
His manners were just *Christian*, —
Becomin' meek and mild,
And he loved each rough-neck miner
Like a mother loves her child.

69. George Winkler. *Songs Unbidden* (Victoria: Victoria Printing & Publishing, 1920).

If one of us was ailin'
He'd take his pack and hike
To that cabin in the mountains
Where illness chanced to strike,
And he never thought of leavin'
Till all was right and well: —
And that's why most us miners won't
Meet Father Pat in hell.

He died: we built a monument
At Rossland, on the hill,
And many sun-burned prospectors
Chipped in to pay the bill;
And when I look upon it
A great big tear-drop starts; —
But it's nothin' to the monument
He built within our hearts.

— GEORGE WINKLER

On the West Kettle River Road[70]

This is the old log stopping place
Where Gorman West held sway
Abandoned now and gone to waste
Since Gorman passed away.[71]

And here the ancient dining room
Where hungry men were fed
And in this Bar they looked upon
The wine when it was red

And passed their nights in drink and
    play
And when the time seemed long
They put their poker chips away
And raised their voice in song

And each in singing took his part
They sang familiar lays
The old, old songs that touch the heart
Recalling bygone days

And when each singer's song was done
All took up the refrain
And in full-throated unison
They roared it out again

And Father Pat within this room
With ready wit enticed
Many a mining man to come
And hear the words of Christ

The peaceful flowing river winds
The stately spruces through
And few remain of olden times
That Gorman's hostel knew

Now motor cars the roads infest
And strangers speed their ways
But Father Pat and Gorman West
Belong to other days.

— GEORGE WINKLER

70. George Winkler. *Songs of the Okanagan. The Okanagan Historical Society* *of Vernon, BC Annual Report,* 1944.
71. Gorman West died in Greenwood in 1912 at the age of 68. Today little is remembered of him.

In 1879 William Ridley, D. D. (1836–1911), was consecrated the first bishop of the Anglican diocese of Caledonia and sent to Metlakatla, where he lived some twenty years. Conflict soon developed between Ridley and William Duncan, Metlakatla's lay missionary. As a result, Duncan took his followers to Alaska to establish a new community.[72] Ridley translated the New Testament into Tsimshean and journeyed by foot, boat, and canoe to bring the Gospel to regions as far afield as the Queen Charlotte Islands, the Stikine, the headwaters of the Skeena, and along the Bulkley.

The Start[73]

Keen animation fires the mind,
As sheering from the bank we find
Our trimmed canoe in conflict fierce
With dangerous swirls. Their glances
    pierce
The novice with unreasoning fears,
And mingle wrath with furtive tears.
The towline twangs with doleful note;
Submerged a moment, then afloat,
It skims, it skips in shivering mood,
Tempting the current to a feud.

The sweltering team now breathless
    stand,
Hauling their line in hand o'er hand.
Beyond us frowns a matter mass

Of tangled driftwood none can pass.
Five-acred chine of porcupine
Gaunt, splintered trees as quills com-
    bine
To daunt the boldest towing team,
And force us all to cross the stream.

Cross over, children, we will try;
Cross over, we will make her fly.
Embark with wings; prepare, disrobe;
What if the depths we have to probe!
Survey the current, mark the stretch
Between the banks. Where shall we
    fetch
On yonder strand? Ready, ready!
Lightning strokes; but steady, steady.

72. For the story of Metlakatla see Jean Usher's *William Duncan of Metlakatla: A Victorian Missionary in* *British Columbia* (Ottawa: National Museums of Canada, 1974).

73. William Ridley. *Camp* *Fire Light* (London: Seeley and Co., 1906).

Away, sweet bowman, handsomely;
Veer round her stem right tenderly.
She swings! Strike out; set fast your
   feet;
Make every stroke a stroke complete.

Flash lightning paddles; skill display.
Grunt, grunt in unison, hooray!
O carry a rainbow all the way,
From swell to whirl with upflung spray!
                                    — WILLIAM RIDLEY, D. D.

Dublin-born Capt. John Martley (1828–1896) was a veteran of the Crimean War. He received a military land grant in BC when he arrived with his family in 1861. He farmed and built a home, "The Grange," on Pavilion Mountain. He was politically active, was appointed Justice of the Peace for Lillooet in 1878, and was aide-de-camp to the Marquis of Lorne when he visited BC as governor-general in the early 1880s. Under the pseudonym of Erl Viking, Martley authored a book of poems, *Songs Of The Cascades*.

In early 1892, he learned that Father Chirouse had caused an Aboriginal girl to be flogged. Martley, outraged, laid charges against the priest. The case created some controversy and many civic leaders supported Father Chirouse. According to Bishop Lemmens: "It has been a recognized thing that the Indians should be allowed to keep their strict moral code and the punishments inflicted for infraction of the same. The idea of whipping for certain offences is also very common, and I know that Dr. Powell [Superintendant of Indian Affairs] has tacitly approved of it, as has the Indian department here also."[74] The editor of the *Daily Colonist* agreed: "At Metlahkahtla . . . whipping under the direction of the Council and missionary in charge was an ordinary form of punishment . . . [U]nder the old Colonial Government the hands of the missionary were strengthened by the frequent appearance of a ship of war, and the Indians were often compelled to submit to edicts of the missionary and rules of the Council which, if tested at any time, could not have been justified by the law."[75]

---

74. *Daily Colonist*, May 6, 1892.   75. *Daily Colonist*, July 5, 1892.

Martley disagreed, took pen in hand and wrote a poem satirizing a devout Irish Catholic's point of view:

> At Lillooet, British Columbia, on 3rd May, 1892, the Rev. Chirouse, Roman Catholic Priest, was tried before the Hon. Clement Francis Cornwall, County Court Judge, for having caused a young Indian girl to be stripped of her chemise and publicly — i.e., in presence of the tribe — flogged with a rawhide whip; he was convicted and sentenced to be imprisoned for one year. A point was reserved — a mere piece of professional by-play; it was never argued. The Minister of Justice at Ottawa and the provincial Attorney General were both Roman Catholics, and a pardon was secured. It would be interesting to know what representations were made to His Excellency the Governor General. The Catholic vote is a great power in Canada; and, after all — it was only an Indian girl.

Mr. Doolan's Lament[76]

I

Tare an' ages thin, Corny! what's this that yez tell?
Be Saint Pathrick 'tis tirrible news!
Had thim Lillooet boys no rishpict onto Hell
When they shut up good Father Chirouse?

II

'Tis mesilf would have loiked to have been in the Coort,
He'd an iligant laryer ye say?
Oi'd have given MacPh___lips[77] me harty suppoort
Av he'd wanted a foighter that day.

---

76. Erl Viking. *Songs of the*   (London: Horace Cox, 1894).
Cascades. First part.

III

An' for batin' a gurl they throied that good praist! —
Did yez iver hear tell of the loike?
Shure it's proud *we'd* have been, not vexed in the laist,
Av he'd shtruck us, now wouldn't we, Moike?

IV

Obsarve this, me frinds, it don't matther a shtraw
If his Riv'rince was wrong or was roight,
If they poonish our praisthood for brakin' the law,
Shure it's plain that 'tis done out of shpoite.

*Mr. Doolan visiteth New Westminster City; on returning to
Lillooet he discourseth further as follows:*

What tuk place at Weshtminsther Oi'll shortly ralate —
'Tis a roisin' young town be the say —
Shure MacP. is a laryer that cudn't be bate,
He relased the good father to-day. . . .

MacPh__lips, good luck to him, 's troying to prove
The chiefs in ould toimes in thim lands
Used to flog, so his Riv'rince, in marcy and luv,
Was intoitled to lay on *his* hands.

Bad cess to thim hiritics, M__ry__y and all;
But be aisy, me boys, and howld on,
For thim voile parsecuthers 'll crow moighty shmall
Before Davie and honest Sir John.

　　　— ERL VIKING (JOHN MARTLEY)

---

77. McPhillips defended Father Chirouse.

Alexander Maitland Stephen (1882–1942) left Ontario for the West, where he arrived in 1898. His varied career included work as a logger, cowpuncher, Rocky Mountain guide and teacher. He served in WWI and was invalided to Vancouver in 1818. He became a prominent social activist and editor of the *Western Tribune*. He authored several volumes of poetry, two novels, *Classroom Plays for Canadian History*, and edited *The Voice of Canada: Selections of Prose and Verse*. In 1906, he taught school at Rock Creek and no doubt danced a few sets at Carson's.

An Old-Time Dance at Carson's[78]

Night falls in Kettle Valley,
a spangled curtain,
hooked to rocky pinnacles,
rolled over benches
fragrant with sage-brush,
till the river is blurred by dancing stars —
stars that are strong medicine
to fire the blood.

A black fly
on a white wall.
the Camp McKinney stage
crawls along the canyon trail.
Below,
in a patch of timber,
its windows shooting fire,
Carson's cabin
gives it the high-sign.

The driver pulls up short.
"B'lieve there's a dance on
down to Carson's."
He speaks to us
kind o' low and invitin'-like.
"Horses wouldn't mind a rest.
What do you say, boys?"

Say . . . . . . ?
Tune in on an old-time dance!

Ma she met us at the big front door.
"Come in," she sez, "alluz room fer
    more.
There's cake an' chicken an' pie galore.
If there ain't enough, we'll send to the
    store."
A fiddle wailin' like a chained-up dog,
and a piano thumpin' like a love-sick
    frog,

78. A. M. Stephen. *Brown Earth and Bunch Grass* (Vancouver: Wrigley Printing Co., 1931). See Alan Twigg's *Vancouver and Its Writers* (Madeira Park: Harbour Publishing, 1987) for a synopsis of this remarkable man's career.

feet a-shufflin' on the pinewood floors,
the party arrivin' in two's and four's,
sheddin' of wraps, and "How-d'ye-do?"
an' Ma Carson smilin' on the hull
   blame crew!

An' it's "Grand right an' left on the cor-
   ners all,
an' march yer partners down the hall!"
Plump and pretty, in a smilin' row,
the girls sat out if the men were slow.
Then, 'twas, "Swing 'em, boys, an'
   away we go!
Meet yer partner an' pass her by,
an' bow to the lady with the coal-black
   eye!
Gents to the middle, an' jig to the
   fiddle!
Break an' swing!
All-a-man left an' doe-ce-doe,
dance with yer partner, heel an' toe!"

Just home-folks,
Canadian pioneers!
They didn't know about Freud.
When they had a complex, they got rid
   of it.
They didn't swing on the tail of a
   theory.

Under the spangled curtain
of night in the mountains,
like trees in the wind,
they swayed to elemental forces,
touched hands,
whispered together,
shouted, if they felt that way,
and . . . . . .
they were happy.

— ARTHUR MAITLAND STEPHEN

Eliza Jane Swalwell was a mixed-blood Okanagan woman who was born circa 1869. Though many writers have extolled the area's beauty no one has captured the "love of land" more elo-quently than Ms. Swalwell.

This Green and Gracious Land[79]

In the morning it was nice
to ride over the range —
the bunch grass
sunflowers
and lupine
springing up so abundantly
your horse
springing under you at every step
as if he too were enjoying the
promenade
as no doubt he was.

No fences in those days
the bunch grass waving in the wind
like a field of wheat.

Exquisite pleasure to ride —
the green and gracious land stretching for miles
the Sand Rose lying
scattered
on the ground
the sunlight on the hills

I have sometimes seen things
sensed something
so serene and beautiful
it left me weak
and weeping
as I sat in the saddle.

— ELIZA JANE SWALWELL

79. This is a "found" poem taken from Ms. Swalwell's "Girlhood Days in Okan- agan," *The Okanagan Historical Society of Vernon, BC Annual Report*, 1939, p. 37.

Orchards frothing with blossoms or spangled with fruit have inspired generations of poets. The vast Okanagan orchards were the most renowned in BC, but the Kootenays also had a thriving fruit growing industry. Lloyd Roberts (1884–1966), son of famed poet Sir Charles G. D. Roberts, considered the orchardist's lot.

The Fruit Rancher[80]

He sees the rosy apples cling like flowers to the bough;
He plucks the purple plums and spills the cherries on the grass;
He wanted peace and silence — God gives him plenty now —
His feet upon the mountain and his shadow on the pass.

He built himself a cabin from red cedars of his own;
He blasted out the stumps and twitched the boulders from the soil;
And with the axe and chisel he fashioned out a throne
Where he might dine in grandeur off the first-fruits of his toil.

His orchard is a treasure-house alive with song and sun,
Where currants ripe as rubies gleam and golden pippins glow;
His servants are the wind and rain whose work is never done
Till winter rends the scarlet roof and banks the halls with snow.

He shouts across the valley and the ranges answer back;
His brushwood smoke at evening lifts a column to the moon;
And dim beyond the distance where the Kootenai snakes black,
He hears the silence shattered by the laughter of the loon.
      — LLOYD ROBERTS

80. A. M. Stephen, ed. *Voice of Canada* (Toronto: J. M. Dent & Sons, 1926).

Fred Nash (1855–1940) journeyed from Ontario to California, where he lived until he felt an urge to move northward. Somewhere along the way, he acquired a horse, Jack, and by 1897 their wanderings had taken them to Dog Creek, which flowed into the western shore of the Arrow Lakes. "This is the place I have dreamed of and this is going to be our home," Fred told Jack. In fine partnership, Fred and Jack cleared the land. Fred planted an orchard, a garden, and a profusion of flowers, which he loved. Fred and Jack worked together until 1913, when Jack became ill and did not recover. Fred buried Jack in the rose garden in front of the house and wrote a poem.

In 1907 Nash's acreage was purchased by a developer, subdivided, sold as orchard land and renamed Renata. The community's 150 residents formed a co-op, built an irrigation system (forming pipes by boring holes through logs), and a sawmill, which enabled them to make their own fruit boxes. Renata flourished until the late 1960s.

Under the Columbia River Treaty, the river was dammed. The Arrow Lakes rose and flooded all the villages along the shore: Syringa Creek, Deer Park, Broadwater, Edgewood, Burton, Carrol's Landing, Graham's Landing, Arrow Park, Glendevan, Shoreholme, St. Leon, Arrowhead, and Renata. Residents were forced to abandon their homes. Their orchards and buildings were flattened by tractors, heaped into pyres, and razed. In 1969, the gates of the Hugh Keenleyside Dam closed and the rising waters crept over what once had been Renata.

Poem by Fred Nash[81]

Over the mountain trails we tramped
Good old Jack and I.
Out in the woods by night we camped
Beneath the starlit sky.

It was not gold I hoped to stake
My quest was land by stream or lake
And the still waters by.

81. Mary Warkenton and Rose Ann Rohn. *The Story of* *Renata 1887-1965* (Renata: self-published, 1965).

My dream was of a valley farm
Where fruit trees would grow
And the distant mountains lending
  charm
With their crests of snow.

On the Arrow Lakes I found the spot
And blessed the fates that cast my lot
Where the waters flow.

We had land to clear and then to break
Fruit trees to plant and fence to make
As the years rolled by.
Buildings went up amid the wood
Where once roamed the bear.
Fruit trees bloomed where firs had stood
Cherry, peach and pear.

Jack was only a horse 'tis true
But I loved him well.
All that a horse might know Jack knew
And he did excel.

He worked with me to till the soil,
He shared with me the fruits of toil
And what else befell.

Now he sleeps by my roses there
His bridle layed by
He needs not now my daily care
So musing, I sigh.

I'll hear no more his welcome neigh
He'll share no more my working day.
Goodbye, old Jack, Goodbye.

— FRED NASH

Eric Duncan (1862–1944), farmer, poet, and philosopher, was born in the Shetland Islands. He was an early settler in the Comox Valley and developed a flourishing farm. His published reminiscences and observations included *From Shetland to Vancouver Island*, *The Rich Fisherman*, *Fifty-seven Years in the Comox Valley*, *The Sheep Thief*, and a book of poetry, *Rural Rhymes*. In his introduction to *Rural Rhymes*, Duncan stated that the rhymes "are not the rose-tinted reveries of a rusticated rhapsodist, but the regular, rough reminiscences of a real rancher, written by himself." In December 1896, the *Province*'s reviewer read the poems. He was not kind, deeming that Duncan's "lines on 'Drought' are entitled to better company than the miserable farm-yard doggerel which precedes them."

Drought[82]

August returns, but not with plenty crowned;
Thin, dwarfed, and light of head is all the grain.
The meagre hay was, ere its blossom, browned;
The root crops withered, all for want of rain.
The cows for aftergrass do seek in vain,
And through the boundless woods afar they roam.
They anger me; but when driven home again
Their sad eyes plead for hay, and I am dumb,
For I have none to spare — I think of months to come.
    — ERIC DUNCAN

An Ox Song[83]

I have an ox, a good work ox,
Steady to plough or draw;
Not vicious he, his only fault
Is kleptomania.

He has a long and lanky frame,
His belly nought can fill,
Yea, should he gulp a bale of hay
He would be lanky still. . . .

One dawn I found him trampling
   through
My heaviest field of grain;
All night he had been toiling there
To fill himself — in vain.

I tied him to the broken fence,
A crab-tree switch I tore

(For I was mad), and thrashed him as
He ne'er was thrashed before.

He took it full patiently,
He knew it was his due,
But yet at me, when loosing him,
A spiteful look he threw —

A look which said, as plain as speech,
"My hide is disarranged,
Oh-h-h! but I will remember this,
And I will be revenged."

Next night when I in peaceful bunk
Did comfortably snore,
Roused by a raging storm of bells,
I sprang upon the floor. . . .

82. Eric Duncan. *Rural Rhymes* and *The Sheep Thief*. Microfiche No. 14936. (Montreal: Canadian Institute for Historical Microreproductions).

83. Ibid.

No time for socks, I quickly plunged
Barefoot into my boots,
And, lighted by the round-faced moon,
Sped fast through bush and roots.

Oho! they fill the turnip field,
Cows gobbling all they can;
But see the huge, ungainly form
That lumbers in their van!

The moon, the calm, indifferent moon,
My frenzied fury mocks,
As round and round the fields I tear
After that dreadful ox.

I cleared the place, but not before
The crop was half destroyed;
Now many a night-alarm have I,
And many an hour employed

In mending gaps, for though no more
That ox will wander free,
The cows, through his example, are
Almost as bad as he.

But I have seen the foolishness
Of trifling with a thief,
And so this good but erring ox
Will very soon be beef.

— ERIC DUNCAN

Although surrounded by the beautiful landscapes and fertile soil
of the Comox Valley, Eric Duncan often succumbed to home-
sickness for his birthland — the bleak Shetland Islands.

Unreasonable[84]

There, islands overhung by sullen skies
Lie lone amid the ever-moaning main;
There naked hills and cliffs enormous rise
Which tireless winds and waves assault in vain
Scant soil returns the toiler meagre gain,
And pastures thin, with star-like daisies gemmed,
Serve tiny cows, which tethering bonds restrain
From oatfields small and poor, by peat-moss hemmed, —
    A bleak and stormy land, to scarcity condemned.

And here, by mountains sheltered, and by trees,
A winding valley opens far along;
Here the height-sweeping storm becomes a breeze,
The cascade's distant plunge a drowsy song.

---

84. Eric Duncan. *The Rich Fisherman* (London: Century, 1910).

Here flocks and herds wax frolicsome and strong
On Nature's wild profusion, broadly sown,
The cows, that up the river pathway throng,
Their cumbrous udders feelingly bemoan —
    A land of rural bliss, to poverty unknown.

Yet, oh, swift river, could thy course be mine!
Yet, oh, strange heart, still yearning wistfully
Oh restless eyes, that range the rugged line
Of peaks majestic, longing for the sea; —
That low, dull stretch of uniformity
Which laps the solemn strand where I was born —
Grey Shetland! Thy grim spell takes hold of me,
Here dwell I, right by Amalthea's[85] horn,
    Grandeur and joy around, yet inwardly forlorn.

        — ERIC DUNCAN

The Doukhobors are a Christian sect that originated in Russia and practiced pacifism and non-violence.[86] In Russia, they were persecuted and tortured for resisting conscription into the army and for refusing to pay taxes used for war. In 1895, their leader, Peter Verigin, ordered them to demonstrate their pacifism by burning every weapon they could find. The Cossacks' brutal response to "the burning of the guns" hastened the Doukhobors' planned migration to Canada, where they hoped to find religious freedom. Many settled in the Kootenays, where they lived communally and developed extensive orchards and farmlands. Peter Diachkoff, who had participated in the burning of guns, composed a hymn to commemorate the event.

---

85. I.e., cornucopia; horn of plenty.
86. For an excellent account of the Doukhobor story, see George Woodcock's *The Doukhobors* (Toronto: Oxford University Press, 1968).

The Burning of the Guns[87]

Let us recall, brethren, our struggle
Why we had to leave our homes;
'Twas for truth they drove us out;
Pains, for faith in Christ, we bore.

Chorus:
'Twas for truth they drove us out;
Pains, for faith in Christ, we bore.

We recognized our Saviour's pathway
And perceived His universal love;
For the cause of truth and freedom
We have had to shed our blood. . . .

Chorus:
[Last two lines of each stanza are
  repeated.]

With His love, forever inspiring,
He told us, foes, to love;
So, our weapons we discarded,
Human life we'd take no more.

The words of Christ we valued highly,
Murderous deeds we wished to avoid;
We built a bonfire of our weapons
Which burned in the field late at night.

The flames kept devouring the weapons,
Columns of smoke rose up toward the sky;
Some guns discharged in the fire,
Making their loud echoes heard far and
  wide.

Brethren and sisters did assemble
And sang their prayers to our Father
  above;
Suddenly a detachment of Cossacks
  appeared
And prepared for battle.

Fully one hundred of these mounted
  Cossacks
Speedily raced to our group gathered
  'round;
Their captain, named Praga, like a
  murderous chieftain
Shouted to his horsemen "Hurrah!"

Then it was as if a whirlwind
Had attacked our people;
Praga wished to trample us down
With the hooves of his horses.

Lash after lash on our backs kept
  descending.
The whistle of whips only was heard;[88]
With blood we all were spattered,
But we kept closing our ranks even
  tighter. . . .

All our weapons burned completely.
Only a memory of them remains.
Guns and sabres of all assortments
Became one bulky, leaden mass.

---

87. Kenneth Peacock. *Songs of the Doukhobors*. (Ottawa: National Museum of Canada. Bulletin No. 231, 1970).

88. ". . . [M]ounted Cossacks . . . beat them with their lead-tipped whips." Peacock, op. cit.

Whoever was a soldier at that time
Refused to serve in the army;
They were all jailed and tortured
And exiled to Siberia.

As punishment the villages
Were placed under surveillance by the
  authorities;

And the shameful deeds committed by
  the Cossacks
Are too numerous to recount.

In humility, in meekness,
We put an end to evil;
Now we live in prayer;
Christ is our Tsar, God is our Father.

            — PETER DIACHKOFF

In the 1890s, Slocan was the service centre for the numerous silver/lead mines springing up in the area. The hectic prosperity in the "Silvery Slocan" drew crowds of migrants. Not all were welcome, as an item in the *Slocan Drill* attests: "Slocan is, and has been for sometime, over run with a choice line of vags, bums, stiffs, beggars, fakirs, and other undesirable characters, and it is about time the authorities took action to rid the town of their presence. No less than nine of these beauties, who had been ordered out of Sandon by the authorities, showed up here in one day." These comments inspired poet Robert T. Anderson, "The Kipling of the Kootenays" (1880–1960) to pen a few verses.

Anderson lived in Lemon Creek and, barely out of his teens, contributed numerous poems to newspapers in the Kootenays. He moved to Edmonton, where he became a fireman, served in France during WWI, and spent the remainder of his life in Edmonton.

Weary Willie's Ordeal[89]

He had travelled every inch of ground
From Palouse down to Frisky;
Had ridden upon a brake-beam
Till he found it kind of risky.
He had been a Weary Willie
Since his travelling days began,
But they tagged him as a vagrant
When he landed in Slocan.

He had counted every railroad tie
The Yankee lines can boast,
By Seattle and Tacoma,
And the towns along the coast.
But they ran him out of Nelson
So beneath Misfortune's ban,
He had hoofed it on the CPR
Along toward Slocan.

His clothes were somewhat seedy,
And his hair was rather long,
His beard unkempt and tangled,
His breath a trifle strong.
And he always wore a coat of dirt
Above a coat of tan;
But they spoke of "unwashed presence"
When he landed in Slocan.

The ad that's for the Wilson House,
It seems intended for:
"Most any trail into the town
Will lead you by our door;

And if you're dry" — that caught him,
When he that ad did scan,
He thought that it was Paradise,
In Silvery Slocan.

He humped it on by Lemon Creek,
With two ties at a stride —
The only time he never thought
That they were placed too wide.
But though he hit a trail all right,
That to the city ran,
They shoved him in the Bastille,
When he landed in Slocan.

They put him in the cooler —
But that was no disgrace —
The only thing that hurt him
Was when he washed his face.
They gave him soap and water
And hunted up a pan,
And the hobo's heart was broken
In Silvery Slocan.

There's lots of stiffs about the town,
But ever, without fail,
They all turn into Christie's[90] stiffs
When they are in the gaol.
We've beggars, vags, and bums galore,
But trust now, every man,
It won't be many moons before
They all vamoose Slocan.

---

89. Robert T. Anderson. *The Old Timer and Other Poems* (Edmonton: Edmonton Printing & Publishing Co., 1909). He also published *Canadian Born & Other Western Verse* (Edmonton: Esdale Press, 1913).

So all you genial hoboes,
That love to hit the track,
Just turn your faces southward
Again, and mosey back;

For, to all but honest workingmen
It's far the safest plan.
To keep about a hundred miles
Between them and Slocan.

— ROBERT T. ANDERSON

Excitement rippled through the mining camps of the East Kootenays when it was learned that Lord and Lady Aberdeen would visit the gold fields around Rossland. No "Weary Willies" they, and "Mountaineer" composed a paean of welcome:

Welcome to Lord and Lady Aberdeen[91]

O'er the ocean, up the lakes and rivers,
Through the hills and forests, comes the noble
Earl of Aberdeen with message from her
Gracious Majesty the Queen. . . .

Then come from
Bonnie Scotland, come from Windsor Castle,
Ireland's friend and helper. Come, seventh
Earl of House of Aberdeen; come, come
Herald of the Queen. . . .

Come, o'er Rocky Mountains, thro' the Selkirk
Ranges and the Arrow Lakes, in bosom
Of great cliffs and canyons; come to mountain
Gorges, view our life of pleasure.

Man is
Never lonely standing on the benches
Of the mountains with all gifts of God in
Nature ever at his service.

90. Provincial Constable
Christie.

91. *Daily Colonist,*
November 25, 1895.

                    Who can
Cease to love the mountains? emblems of
Great convulsions in the globe we stand on.
Love them for their beauty, love them for their
Grandeur, love them for their wonder; ay, for
Something less deserving — for their gold and
Silver, heaved up thro' great fissures made by
Gases in the lakes and lab'rinths, held by
Only three leagues deep of solid matter.
But the gold is precious for its beauty;
Ay, and for its use — for it "answers
All things." Hence the hill that yields it, we fall
Down and worship.

                    'Tis not here in sands and
Shoals all drifted by the winds, the tides and
Freshets, but is housed in solid rocks, now
Standing without limit, for all the world
To flock to, as shrine of worship!

                    Come, then,
Visit this our hamlet, weak in numbers,
But rich in gifts the gods have kept through
Ages, to be servants at a time most
Needed.

        And if 'tis thy wont, like to the
Inca king of old, come, noble Earl of
Aberdeen, come now, and fill a spacious
Room with gold.
        — MOUNTAINEER[92]

92. Rossland resident David Glass.

Unfortunately, the vice-regal party did not make the planned stopover at Rossland or hear the words of welcome, and in Victoria a correspondent expressed his thoughts on "Mountaineer's" poetic offering:[93]

Well, I'll be blow'd, if since I have been here,
I have read lines like those the Mountaineer
Had publish'ed in the *Colonist* of yest-
Erday, upon the subject of the guest
They wanted for to catch but couldn't do
So; for Lord Aberdeen went right straight through.

And I expect he'll break his heart because
He couldn't stop or tarry, stay or pause
At any town productive of such cheer-
Full poetry as that of "Mountaineer."
    — MUDLARK

Robert Thornton Lowery (1859–1921) came to BC from his native Ontario in 1891. In 1893, he was in Kaslo, where he published his first BC newspaper, the *Kaslo Claim*. Unfortunately, in 1892 the banks in Spokane, the financial centre for the Kootenays, went bankrupt, and so did the *Claim*. The final edition was printed on August 25, 1893. The front page bore an outline of a tombstone on which was inscribed: "Sacred to the Memory of *The Kaslo Claim*. Born May 12, 1893, Died August 25, 1893. Age — 16 Weeks. Let Her R.I.P." Under the tombstone was a Lowery poem:

This monument upon the Primal page,
Speaks in sad words of the impending
    gloom,
Tells of the battles that the Claim did
    wage
To save the town of Kaslo from the tomb.

But all its loyal efforts are as naught,
Its pennant now is trailing in the dust,
By the financial flurry it was caught,
And like the town of Kaslo it is "BUST."
    — ROBERT THORNTON
    LOWERY

93. *Daily Colonist*, November 26, 1895.

Undaunted, Lowery went on to publish the *Nakusp Ledge*, the *Ledge*, the *Kaslo Claim* (relocated), the *Paystreak*, *Golden Claim*, *Slocan Drill*, *Claim*, *Ozonogram*, the *Nugget*, *Float*, and *Similkameen Star*.[94] Near the end of 1894 Lowery decided to move the *Nakusp Ledge* to New Denver, where it became, simply, *The Ledge*. He frequently chastised subscribers and advertisers who were slow to pay. Postal authorities twice refused to allow his newspapers to go through the mails because they offended "against decency and good morals."

Printer's Poetry[95]

Lives of poor men oft remind us
Honest toil won't stand a chance.
The more we work, there grow behind us
Bigger patches on our pants.
On our pants once new and glossy
Now are stripes of different hue,
All because subscribers linger
And won't pay us what is due.
Let us then, be up and doing.
Send the pay however small,
Or when snows of winter strike us,
We shall have no pants at all.
— ROBERT THORNTON
LOWERY

In 1898, the Canadian government fretted over the large number of Americans thronging to the Klondike. It dispatched the Yukon Field Force, 200 soldiers strong, to fly the Union Jack and to help the North West Mounted Police maintain Canadian law. In January 1898, the minister of the interior, anxious to develop "All-Canadian" routes to the gold fields, announced that he had signed a contract for construction of a wagon road and railway from Telegraph Creek to Teslin Lake. The wagon road would be built in six weeks; the railroad would quickly follow. He envisioned the miner taking a steamboat from Vancouver or Victoria to Wrangell (3 days), a paddlewheeler up the Stikine to Telegraph

94. For an account of Lowery's colourful career see Bronson A. Little's "Robert T. Lowery: Editor, Publisher and Printer" in *BC Historical News*, Spring 1998, pp. 18-23.

95. *The Ledge*, November 26, 1903.

Creek (2 days), the railroad to Teslin Lake (1 day), and a steamboat to Dawson (7 days).

To avoid high steamboat fares, the miner could take the Ashcroft Trail ("The Poor Man's Route"). Starting at Ashcroft, he could follow old trails to the Cariboo, where the abandoned Collins telegraph line would lead him to Telegraph Creek and the Teslin railway. The *British Columbia Mining Record*, although pessimistic about the greenhorn's chances of success, assured him that "The country from Telegraph Creek to Teslin is flat and easily travelled, and pack trains can be hired at the former place at relatively reasonable rates. Beyond this point a good trail will be open next year . . . indeed, a fair trail exists there even now."[96]

By the hundreds, miners and pack animals struggled over the gruelling trail to Telegraph Creek. Horses and mules plunged through bogs, sprawled over windfalls, slid on slimy rocks and roots. Most collapsed from lack of food and exhaustion and were abandoned to wolves and starvation.[97] Scurvy-ridden trekkers drowned fording rivers or falling through ice; some starved, others froze to death. Hamlin Garland, one of the stampeders, recalled his journey.

In the Cold Green Mountains[98]

In the cold green mountains where the
   savage torrents roared,
And the clouds were gray above us,
And the fishing eagle soared,
Where no grass waved, where no
   robins cried,
There our horses starved and died,
In the cold green mountains.

In the cold green mountains,
Nothing grew but moss and trees,
Water dripped and sludgy streamlets
Trapped our horses by the knees.
Where we slipped, slid, and lunged,
Mired down and wildly plunged
Toward the cold green mountains!
   — HAMLIN GARLAND

96. *British Columbia Mining Record*, January, 1898.
97. For a comprehensive account of the Klondike gold rush, see Pierre Berton's *Klondike* (Toronto: McClelland & Stewart, 1977).
98. Hamlin Garland. *The Trail of the Goldseekers* (New York: Macmillan, 1899).

All along the trail, on notepaper and blazed trees, were written notes of despair: "Where the hell are we?" "Poison weeds ahead." And beside abandoned horses, "If my horse is fit to travel, bring him along." On Groundhog Mountain, wistful words were written on a blaze:

> There is a land of pure delight
> Where grass grows belly high;
> Where horses don't sink out of sight;
> We'll reach it by and by.

The ragged and worn men who reached Telegraph Creek faced another crushing blow. There was no railway to Teslin nor would one be built. The Senate had balked at the contractor's terms and refused to pass the bill. Work on the promised wagon road had also been abandoned, and logs that were cut to bridge the bogs had sunk into the mire. The scarlet-coated Yukon Field Force, 200 strong and accompanied by four nurses and a female correspondent, had pre-empted all available packers (including Cataline) and pack animals. Norman Lee's[99] 200 head of cattle that he hoped to sell at Telegraph Creek (but couldn't — by then Telegraph Creek was nearly deserted) plodded on, stripped the Teslin Trail of what little forage there was and churned the route into a slithery, sucking, swamp. Some 230 km had to be traversed to reach Teslin Lake, then another 920 km to Dawson City. Many lost heart and turned back, defeated. The list of suicides grew longer. Only the most grimly determined pushed on.

A sentiment shared by all was etched on a blazed tree.[100]

> Damn the journey, Damn the track
> Damn the distance there and back.
> Damn the sunshine, Damn the weather,
> Damn the goldfields altogether!

---

99. Gordon Elliot, ed. *Klondike Cattle Drive* (Vancouver: Mitchell Press, 1960).

100. Brereton Greenhous. *Guarding the Goldfields. Canadian War Museum Historical Publication No. 24* (Toronto: Toronto and Oxford Dundurn Press, 1987).

Years later an RCMP officer travelling in the Skeena headwaters came across traces of a poem and drawings which had been inscribed on a blazed hemlock with a knife and indelible pencil. The drawings were placed between the stanzas. The poem was rescued from oblivion by Marious Barbeau, as recounted in his "The Poor Man's Trail" in *Canadian Geographic Journal*, July 1934.

The Poor Man's Trail

This is the pan of virgin gold
From the Klondyke River swift and cold
Found by a northern miner bold,
And by him to a steamboat owner sold.

This is the editor, false and cute,
Who said it was proved byond dispute
By evidence no one could refute
That the best way in was "The Poor
    Man's Route."

This is the steamboat owner, sly,
Who wanted his boats to the north to ply,
And so brought over the honest (?) P.-I.[101]
And ran his rates up ever so high.

This is the Poor Man, innocent fool,
Who never went to a lying school,
And so was willing to be the tool
Of selfish liars, false and cruel.

---

101. Seattle's *Post-Intelli-gencer*. Spokane merchants were anxious to cash in on the outfitting business and boosted the advantages of the Ashcroft Trail.

This is the place where those men will go
Who swindled innocent people so,
Robbing them of their hard-earned
  dough,
And giving them only Mud and Snow.
      — UNKNOWN

This is the grave that the poor man fills,
After he died from fever and chills,
Caught while tramping the Stikine hills,
Leaving his wife to pay up his bills.

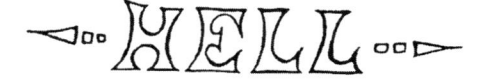

Until the Grand Trunk Pacific was completed in 1914, Skeena River sternwheelers were the only lines of communication between Prince Rupert and Hazelton, the head of navigation. With winter freeze-up, dog teams had to be used to carry mail to scattered northern communities. In 1910, while Sperry "Dutch" Cline[102] was sledding mail along the Skeena, he composed some verses entitled "Mush, You Malemutes, Mush." Over the years, other mushers, including Pete Curran, contributed a verse or two, some in Chinook. By 1950, the verses lived only in the memory of a Mr. Saul of Burns Lake, and he remembered but a few of them. Lyster "Barney" Mulvaney, a colourful pioneer credited with founding Burns Lake, had a mail contract in those early years. He obtained the verses from Saul and rescued them from oblivion.

102. See Cecil Clark's "Sergeant Sperry Cline, Frontier Policeman" in *Pioneer Days in British* *Columbia, Vol. 4* (Surrey: Heritage House, 1979). Cline reminisces about his mail-carrying days in W. O'Neill, W. J. S. Cline and G. Robinson, *Along the Totem Trail* (Kitimat: Northern Sentinel Press, 1961).

Mush, You Malemutes, Mush[103]

The soft, wet snow was falling fast
As up the Skeena River passed
A youth, with six dogs on the trail
Who bore along King George's Mail.
Mush, you Malemutes, Mush.

His head was bare, his whiskers long,
He cursed in many a different tongue,
His snowshoes lagged, his back was bent
Plumb tired out, but on he went.
Mush, you Malemutes, Mush.

He reached a cabin built of logs,
A woman cried, "Get out, you dogs,
And hurry, now, give me my mail,
If you haven't lost it on the trail."
Mush, you Malemutes, Mush.

"What, none from Mother in the lot?
You've been drunk as like as not
And didn't tell them my first name."
But soft and low the answer came,
Mush, you Malemutes, Mush.

He cracked his whip and on he sped,
A raging torrent just ahead,
An avalanche came down behind
But rid of her, he did not mind.
Mush, you Malemutes, Mush.

A lonely cabin, more delay
He heard another woman say
"Curses on you and your dogs
You brought no Eaton's catalogues,"
Mush, you Malemutes, Mush.

He climbed a hill and stopped again
And spelled aloud each Bohunk[104] name
Lashed on his load and licked a dog
Then hurried on midst snow and fog.
Mush, you Malemutes, Mush.

Fresh snow came down, new trail to
    break,
With many travellers in his wake.[105]
"We've waited hours for you to come
Our snow shoe filling's on the bum."
Mush, you Malemutes, Mush.

A Che Chaco gazed upon his sleigh,
"Imagine handling Mail that way
Why don't he bring a load each day.
I'll report to Laurier right away."
Mush, you Malemutes Mush.

The ice gives away, he plunges through
In current strong beneath the snow.
He fights like mad and gains the shore
Then hikes along the trail once more.
Mush, you Malemutes, Mush.

— SPERRY "DUTCH" CLINE

---

103. See Barney Mulvaney's "The Mailman of the Skeena," *Northwest Digest*. January, 1953.

104. A derogatory term for a Russian or Eastern European.

105. Breaking trail over fresh snowfall was an arduous task; travellers usually took turns taking the lead.

Dogsled in Blackwater Canyon BC ARCHIVES NA-04934

Mulvaney records that "For some reason Pete Curran was not so popular at the Missions . . . but all the rest of the Mail Carriers received a welcome." Pete Curran's contribution follows:

His clothes are wet, his face is froze
No feeling in his hands nor toes,
He gains a Mission, dark and drear.
The preacher cries, "You can't stop
  here."
Mush, you Malemutes, Mush

In the morn they find him on the road
Lying dead beside his load

With glassy stare fixed on the trail
As if to say "I dare not fail."
Mush, you Malemutes, Mush.

There in the twilight, cold and gray,
Lifeless but beautiful he lay.
'Twas not the hardships of the trail
But folk ungrateful for their mail.
Mush, you Malemutes, Mush.

Curran, an experienced trapper and woodsman, was last seen near Hazelton, following a trail up the Skeena and over to the Stikine. Years later an RCMP constable on his way from Telegraph Creek to the Liard found Pete's body in an old trapper's cabin. He had evidently died of starvation.

The Pollon family came to the Peace River country in the 1920s. They built a store / stopping house / post office at Lone Star, Alberta, all of which floundered in the Great Depression. They pulled up stakes and, as Earl recalled, "We ended up with three horses, the rattle-trap wagon, an old coal-oil lantern, a used scythe, and innumerable promissory notes but not one dollar in cash. . . . We intended to travel as far as the wagon road extended into the mountains. . . . What better place than one where someone else had once 'hoped'?"[106] And so the Pollons arrived at Hudson's Hope — the end of the road. In those hardscrabble days, Earl turned his hand to a few more or less ill-fated ventures. Between paying jobs he prospected and ran trap lines. In a remote trapper's cabin, Earl found his muse when, after one exceptionally hard day, he had supper and "sat back, lost in thought. Slowly, words and phrases came to me and by evening's end I had written my first verse."

The Gunthier of this poem was a reclusive man. In the winter he ran a trapline; in the summer he panned for gold. An avid astrologer, he spent hours poring over arcane charts and keeping solitary vigils over the night-time skies.

The Astronomer[107]

Far up on the forks of the Finlay,
The time was quite late in the fall,
When this strange urge came upon him:
He heeded astronomy's call.

Now Gunthier was no Cheechako
He had been through the Chilcoot Pass
We all felt he sure knew better
Than the things he did at the last.

He gathered equipment he needed,
But mostly 'twas books and a thought,
He headed far into the mountains,
Well knowing the dangers he wrought. . . .

Of grub, he took very little;
Snowshoes, he cast them aside;
Climbed far up on the Wolverines,[108]
The North Star used for his guide.

---

106. Earl K. Pollen. *Beneath these Waters* (Hudson's Hope: Hudson's Hope

Publishing Co., n.d.).
107. Ibid.
108. The Wolverine Range

rises between Williston Lake and the Omineca.

He stayed over-long on his journey;
Was missed at the Finlay's small post,
Of which Roy MacDougal was owner
And often had been his host.

Roy organized a search party
To look for Gunthier's cold trail;
They hunted for weeks with departments
But hunted to no avail.

The snows of winter were on them;
They covered his wandering sign.
They would lose it out in the muskegs,
They would find it under a pine.

Finally the deep snows of winter
Completely covered his tracks.
They called in their men and their dogs.
Sadly they all turned back. . . .

Months after they re-started searching;
Now this is a funny thing —
But tracks that are made in the fall
Will show again in the spring.

Finally the searchers found him
At rest by an evergreen tree;
He had frozen or starved by his campfire
With astronomy books on his knees.

High up on the Wolverine Mountains
Does Gunthier still study a star?
Or is he tracking the satellites
And wondering what they are?

— EARL K. POLLON

An economic depression swept over Canada and the US in 1907–08
and threw the nation into a state of insecurity. Owning a piece of
farmland seemed to offer a modicum of security to the scores of
prospective settlers lured to the Queen Charlotte Islands by BC
government pamphlets and developers' brochures extolling the
area's agricultural merits. Historian Kathleen Dalzell writes, "The
radiant offer of good farming land at give-away pre-emption prices
was like manna from heaven. . . . However, the fine print in this
seeming benevolence was that 'unsurveyed' bit-to which should
also have been added 'unmapped.'"[109]

---

109. Kathleen Dalzell. *The Queen Charlotte Islands, Vol.* 1 (Madeira Park: Harbour Publishing, 1993).

The Lament of the Graham Islanders[110]

What is our Island coming to, we ask the passer-by,
Since coal and timber cruisers got their fingers in the pie?
You'll find their stakes from shore to shore, no matter where you go.
And when the farmer comes along he finds his cake's all dough.

When you write down to Victoria about this Island shore
They send you books and papers and pamphlets by the score;
They tell you farming land is good — but they forget to say
That as far as getting it's concerned, you'd better stay away.

These books tell all about the vast amount of farming land
And paint a glowing picture of a future near at hand,
When steamboats come and railroads run, of canneries galore,
Where you can sell your products, all you raise and then some more.

But when the people get here and start to look it o'er,
They find that timber limits run a mile back from every shore;
They find the whole blam'd country staked for coal and oil and tree,
And if they want to get a farm they'll have to stake the sea!

And the sea, as far as that's concerned, is staked for fish and clam
And submarine and Lord knows what — it's just as bad as land.
Oh, take a tip, you land-seekers, and do not wend your way
To Graham Isle to pre-empt; you'll find it does not pay.

The thing that bothers us the most, what we can't understand,
Is why the Gov'ment advertises to settle up the land.
It's like the treacherous lion who'd lure the deer into his lair.
Are they in league with steamboat lines for a rake-off on the fare?

---

110. *Queen Charlotte
Islander*, February 5, 1912,
quoted in Dalzell, op. cit.

I could name men among us who have travell'ed many a mile
On the strength of pamphlets they've got regarding Graham Isle.
And if you don't believe me, come and see; you'll find it so,
For they're still awaiting records on land staked a year ago.

Now it may be just and legal to play this title game
But to those who come and those right here, it's a dirty shame
To encourage people to find land, as I've already said,
With trees staked o'er and coal below, they'd better far be dead!

All east of Masset Inlet was reserved six years ago.
From purchase lease lend and timber then we thought we'd a show;
But now it's covered up with coal and oil lease as well,
And a pre-emptor couldn't get a spoonful if he were to go to H__l!

Oh, yes! the prospect here, my lands, for farms are a fake.
You may as well stay where you are and dream about our stake.
We who are here will linger on and try to live in peace
Until some cruiser comes along and stakes the ducks and geese!
    — ANONYMOUS

Author Peter Trower[111] recalls interviewing George McInnis in 1975 when the long-time logger and poet had recently celebrated his 100th birthday. "I was prepared for incredible decrepitude," Trower recalled, "but he looked no more than a hale eighty. He sat in an armchair, nattily formal in a black suit, hands clasped on a walnut cane. His memory of those long-ago times was remarkably clear."

McInnis, born in Prince Edward Island in 1875, began his logging career in Maine pine camps at age 19. He reached Puget Sound in 1902, worked the Washington woods until 1906 before coming to BC where he spent the rest of his days.

---

111. Trower's articles on McInnis appeared in *BC Logging News*, February 1976; *Vancouver Magazine*, September 1986; and David Day, ed., *Men of the Forest.* Sound Heritage, vol .6, no. 3 (Victoria: Provincial Archives of BC, 1977.

Waiting[112]

(Powell River, Christmas Eve, 1908)
We were sixty men with a six month's stake
Waiting the *Comox* and bound for town
Six months on an island in Powell Lake
All fit as a fiddle and weathered and brown.

Six months of wearisome ten-hour days
and a straw-lined bunk when the day was done
With Sundays to sit on the float and gaze
At the stump-clad hillside and dream of fun. . . .

We were grouped on deck as the dock drew near
(Like exiles back from some land afar)
With our blanket rolls and our working gear,
As we docked astern of the *Cassiar.*
We're docked and the gangplank's over the side
And sounds to the tramp of our eager feet
Now freed from the hampering wind and tide
We're crossing the tracks to Carrall Street.

To Carrall Street and a welcoming hand
From the man at the bar and from friends we know
At the Boulder, Bodega, Europe or Grand
All of us in with stakes to blow.

We're scattering now (we're a group no more)
Each seeking the dream he has nursed so long
The wine is at hand and we've known of yore
That it widens the choice of the women and song.
    — GEORGE MCINNIS

---

112. George McInnis. *Saga of*   (Vancouver: self-published,
the West Coast Loggers   1968).

Straight-grained, strong but light, Sitka spruce wood was deemed essential in the construction of WWI fighter planes. In the Queen Charlotte Islands, where the tree flourished, logging camps sprang up under the auspices of the Imperial Munitions Board. To keep up the morale of the hard-working isolated loggers, the YMCA was contracted to supply recreational facilities. Daniel Hatt (1869–1942) was the "Y" man in 1918. He organized baseball, football as well as boxing matches and kept the recreation hall well provided with crokinole, checkers, cards, a library, and movies twice a week. In his spare time, he wrote a book of poetry.[113] Hatt's observations — and his descriptions of the loggers' craft in those long-ago days before chainsaws — formed the basis of his poems.

Sitka Spruce

Sitka Spruce is fine of grain
And Sitka Spruce is tough,
To carry weight and stand the strain
There grows no better stuff;

It thrives upon Queen Charlotte Isles
And lifts its head on high,

When summer's sun upon it smiles
Or winter rages by.

Sitka Spruce is straight and clear,
And Sitka Spruce is light,
That aviator knows no fear
It girds into the fight.

— DANIEL HATT

The Fallers

Carefully noting the lean of the tree,
Marking the push of the breeze,
Choosing the place for the giant to fall
Among the surrounding trees —

These are the fallers, with saw and axe,
And iron wedge and mall,
Bringing to earth the mighty trunks
No matter how huge and tall.

---

113. Daniel Hatt. *Sitka Spruce-Songs of Queen Charlotte Islands* (Vancouver: R. P. Latt & Co., 1919).

Perched on their spring-boards, sway-
   ing there
To the grating swish of the saw
Eating its way through the heart of the
   tree
Like the teeth of a tireless jaw.
Swinging the axe on the undercut,
Chopping with echoing blow,
Carefully placing the falling wedge —
They are laying the monster low.

Trembling seizes the lofty tree
To the tip of its topmost branch.
With a mighty crack it reels and falls
Through the air like an avalanche,
Crashing down through the lesser
   trees,
Thundering on the earth,
Lying, a giant babe in arms
Of the Mother who gave it birth.
     — DANIEL HATT

Davis rafts "were used to transport logs across the exposed waters off the west coast of Vancouver Island and Queen Charlotte Sound, where conventional booms — used to transport logs on protected waters — could not withstand the larger swells and rougher waves of the open ocean."[114] Assembling these log rafts was a lengthy, complex procedure requiring an eight- or nine-man crew. Despite many peoples' optimism, the Davis Rafts were phased out in the 1920s with the use of log barges, which were, in turn, replaced in the 1950s by self-dumping log barges.

Today little is known of poet Robert H. Chestnut (1875–1940), who was struck by the ingenuity of the rafts' construction.

The Davis Raft[115]

Along this Coast where trees grow tall,
Where their girths are in excess,
There are perils of the Ocean,
Which subdue man more or less.
So, to tow his logs in safety
To the mills and lumber craft,

There was devised a simple fabric
Known as the Davis Raft.

Bert Davis, this Raft's founder,
Was a jovial genial pard;
He could tell you of its merits,

114. Ken Drushka in Daniel Francis, ed. *Encyclopedia of British Columbia*, (Madeira Park: Harbour Publishing, 2000).
115. Robert H. Chestnut. *Rambling Rhymes of the BC Coast* (Vancouver: Clarke & Stuart, 1933).

Davis rafts of airplane spruce, Queen Charlotte Islands
BC ARCHIVES NA-07109

By the hour or by the yard.
But when the world was scrapping
And they needed Airplane Spruce,
Then this method of conveying logs
Gained its universal use.
Its founder was particular
To have the bottom made
With special lengths of logs,
Each by steel cables laid.
These securely held to side sticks
By clamps, and shackles strong,
Made a cradle of security,
Through stormy waters long.

By steam into this cradle
Logs are rolled tier on tier;
And joined endwise together
They allay the towman's fear.
Then, with logs enough assembled
To give the top a rounded form,
More cables bind the whole in place
To weather sea or storm.
In million feet, by more or less,
Of timbers' measured store,
Are logs in cables' steel embrace,
Towed safe to distant shore.
Through weather and through waters,

Where the Flat-boom can't survive,
By the use of Davis' Raft
Lumber needs do safe arrive.

Along this Coast where trees are larger,
Where they grow 'long open shore,
This method of conveyance

Will be used more, and still more;
And if built to Davis measure,
Towed well with Towman's craft,
The logger, millman, builder,
Will bless DAVIS and his Raft.

— ROBERT H. CHESTNUT

In BC's early days, its coastline was sparsely dotted with the modest cabins of hand loggers, fishermen, and recluses who illumined their homes by Coleman or coal-oil lamps. These feeble glows often served as beacons for night-time mariners.

John Campbell's Shack[116]

It was on a point of Thurlow Island
That a cozy shack once stood;
And while John Campbell lived there,
There was light, and warmth, and
  wood —
Three things which stand for comfort
On any rocky shore
There was always a welcome for you
As you came near the door.

It was the home of John Campbell,
A man who'd passed the Span;
And who had settled down in comfort
On this little neck o' lan';
And, as his light from out the window

Pierced the darkness round about,
Boats, coming round Hall Point,
Could pass the Isle of Shan
If the light was three to starboard,
And the course kept like a man.

But now — this shack is falling down
From neglect and decay;
And the body of John Campbell
Is layed in rest away.
But the soul of he who builded,
Where his light was good to all,
Hovers round the crumbling timbers
And the alders growing tall.

— ROBERT H. CHESTNUT

116. Ibid.

Rev. John Antle was appalled by the number of loggers injured by accidents in the BC woods. With no doctors or hospitals available, serious cases often had to travel great distances for medical assistance. Many died on the journey or while waiting for transportation. Here was a need to be filled and, in 1904, Antle and his young son voyaged upcoast in a 14-foot dinghy to assess the situation. They reached Rock Bay (on Vancouver Island, north of Campbell River), the site of a Hastings Mill Company camp, on a Sunday. Antle recalled that "the only sound was a sort of subdued roar coming from the saloon, and occasional groans from perhaps fifty or a hundred loggers lying around on the grass, in all stages of intoxication."[117] He noted, too, the prevalence of disease in Native communities, for the missionaries had little or no medical training. When he reported his findings to the Missionary Society they appointed him Superintendent of the Columbia Coast Mission and funded a mission-hospital boat large enough to accommodate the crew, two hospital cots, an operating room, a library and an altar. The Hastings Mill Company built Queen's Hospital at Rock Bay, the centre of coastal logging activity and, in 1905, it was opened by the Victorian Order of Nurses.[118]

Antle published a newspaper, *The Log of the 'Columbia,'* which fostered a sense of community between the isolated logging shows. He invited contributions from his readers, and from their remote camps they responded with newsy articles and poems. A frequent contributor was Mrs. B. E. Ward of Reid Island, one of the few pioneer women who found the time and energy to write about their experiences.

117. Doris Anderson. *The Columbia is Coming!* (Sidney: Gray's Publishing, 1982).

118. Helen Shore provides a detailed study of the hospital in "Cottage Hospitals in British Columbia," *British Columbia Historical News*, Fall 2000.

The Call of the British Columbia Forests[119]

O the columbine bells of gold and red
Droop from the cliff that hangs o'erhead,
And a lisping song, low and clear,
Falls upon your startled ear
As each white barnacle, one by one,
Closes its door from the prying sun.
Beneath, where the purple shadows lie,
You watch the rock-cod swimming by.
As the setting sun the waters gild,
You homeward go, your basket filled;
(Perhaps for many years you'll keep
These treasured jewels of the deep.)

In gathering shadows of the night
The flames leap from the camp-fire
   bright;

On the heated rocks the clams you toss
And cover over with kelp and moss;
And there they simmer, steaming hot,
While you fill up the black teapot.
Stirring some batter in an old tin can,
You cook some cakes in the frying pan.
"Surely, the simple life is best,"
You think, as at last you lie at rest
Between the blankets, on your cedar bed.
With the bright stars shining overhead.
The tent flap closed up snug and tight,
In peaceful slumber you pass the night;
Your faithful dog lone guard does keep,
Beside the camp-fire as you sleep.
                              — MRS. B. E. WARD

The storm-battered west coast of Vancouver Island witnessed scenes of unimaginable terror as ships, pounded by wind and breakers, were inexorably driven onto its rocky, desolate shores. In 1910, the West Coast Lifesaving Trail, today's West Coast Trail, from Victoria to Port Renfrew was slashed through tangles of salal and devil's club to give rescuers (or survivors) a line of communication. On November 10, 1918, the 62-foot purse seiner *Renfrew* foundered on the Nitinat Bar. Thirteen lives were lost. The magazine section of Victoria's *Colonist* published articles about the infamous bar on March 1, 1970 and April 9, 1972. The area became known as the Graveyard of the Pacific.

Rev. Percy E. Willis, who served in "The Graveyard", noted its pressing need for both missionary and medical attention. He published and sold a booklet of verse with all proceeds going "toward

119 *The Log of the "Columbia,"* Vol. II, No. 3, May 1907.

the purchase of a boat for missionary work among the lonely and isolated settlers of those four hundred miles of shore line."[120] Unfortunately, nothing seems to have resulted from his efforts.

The Nitinat Bar

The strong tides run o'er the Nit'nat Bar
Like a mill race out of Hell
And if you wish to brave that bar
You need to know it well.
One Christmas when the works had
  closed
The storm clouds piled o'erhead,
The men were paid, their plans were laid,
"We're going home," they said.
Now the works are up on the Lake-
  shore strip,
And to get to the open sea
You run the race down a narrow place,
Then over the bar to the sea.
So the crowd piled on to the *Merry*
  John —
a seiner strongly knit —
With a laughing curse they cast her off
And into the race they hit.
In each man's belt lay a whole season's
  pay,
In their guts the whiskey tore,
So they faced the sea with a drunken
  glee
And rushed at the bar with a roar.
The big seas piled with a wind that was
  wild
On that ragged western shore,

'Tis a fearsome place where the Nit'nat
  Race
Reels in the ocean's gore.
So the *Merry John* kept coming on
And could not slack her pace —
You can't turn back in that narrow track
You've got to run the race.

The walls slid by on either side,
The breakers coming near,
Until at last they were in it fast
And they had no time to fear.
Then things took place in a short brief
  space
That the watchers on the shore
Had scarce the time ere the ocean
  slime
Had covered the *"Johnny"* o'er.
She bowled o'er the spit and struck in
  the dip
Of the breaker next in the line.
But her keel was caught when the next
  one struck
And she disappeared in the brine.
In the foc's'le peak they struggled weak
Until they were all overcome,
And never a one saw another day's sun
Nor spent his Christmas at home. . . .

120. Rev. Percy E. Willis. *Rambling Rhymes from the*   *Graveyard* (Port Alberni: West Coast Printers, 1933).

So if for a thrill you are wandering still,
Just wait till the tide is high,

Then run the race of that ghastly place,
And you'll run it — or you'll die!

— PERCY E. WILLIS

In the late 1800s, Victoria was the homeport for BC's sealing fleet. The schooners set out in the summer for the Pribilof Islands, the rookeries of the fur seals. Each schooner carried open boats or canoes, manned by a crew of three, which were launched from the schooner at the hunting grounds. Seals were speared or shot then taken to the schooner where they were skinned and the pelts salted. In 1867, when the US purchased Alaska from Russia, the fur seal population was estimated at anywhere from 2 to 5 million, and killing was unrestricted. In 1870, however, the Alaska Commercial Company leased from the US exclusive rights to hunt seals on the Pribilofs — 10,000 a year, with prohibitions against killing females and pups. Disgruntled Canadians sealers had to content themselves with working along the BC coast and outside of the US three-mile limit.

By 1885, memories of the Pribolofs' bounty were luring more and more of them back into American waters where they poached with total disregard of a seal's age or gender. Capt. Victor Jacobson wrote, "We came to the sealing grounds of Mt. St. Elias . . . and the seals were lying all around us as far as the eye could see. I ordered all the boats out and that night we had 199 seals . . . and the next few days the seals were just as plentiful. . . . I had over 900 seals in those five days. My smaller schooner, the *Minnie*, had about 800. Those five days were the highest earnings I ever made. I cleared over $15,000."[121] The US tried to protect the drastically declining herd by claiming exclusive jurisdiction over the entire Bering Sea and sent the cutters *Corwin* and *Rush* to seize foreign vessels entering those waters. In 1886, the *Corwin* captured three BC schooners and imprisoned the captains and

121. Eva Marie Sweeney, "Sealing Days of Capt. Victor Jacobson," Vancouver Maritime Museum.

crew.[122] Britain's protest launched a lengthy, complex series of negotiations, which eventually culminated in the 1911 North Pacific Sealing Convention signed by the United States, Great Britain, Russia and Japan.

Sealing In the Behring Sea[123]

(Air: "Where the
Stormy Waves do Roar")
'Twas a gallant captain who trod the
  deck
Of a craft as tight as could be,
Saying, "I've dollars at stake and a
  catch to make
'Mongst the seals in the Behring See-e-
  ee,
'Mongst the seals in the Behring Sea."

Chorus:
Where the spermaceti whale does spout,
In placid felici-tee,
And sleek looking seals can be seen all
  about
Swimming in the Behring Sea.

Then up spoke the cook so bold
Who had shipped at Victori-ee,
"They shall eat hard tack, till they
  come back
From sealing in the Behring Sea."

One day when many miles from the
  land
The look-out says, says he,
"Why, skipper, here's the Corwin a-
  bearing down fast,
And we're in the Behring Sea."

The schooner was hailed by a gruff
  kind of voice
Crying, "No matter who you may be,
You are forfeited to the U-nited States
For fishing in the Behring Sea."

To cut what could be a long yarn short,
They never parted com-pa-nee
'Til in Ounalaska moored, all as prison-
  ers on board
Charged with sealing in the Behring
  Sea.

Next up will speak bluff Johnny Bull,
Demanding schooners three,
And reparation too, from Uncle Sam,
And an end to monopo-lee-ee
And an end to monopo-lee.
      — ANONYMOUS

---

122. For a study of BC's fur seal industry see Peter Murray, *The Vagabond Fleet* (Victoria: Sono Nis, 1988).

123. *Daily British Colonist*, September 16, 1886.

The heyday of the pulp magazines (the early 1900s) provided a ready market for W. B. "Bertrand" Sinclair (1881–1972).[124] He published numerous short stories, novellas, and fifteen novels, the bulk of which drew on his youthful experiences as a cowboy in Montana. In 1912, he moved to BC and expanded his repertoire to include adventure yarns set in the far north and in the logging and fishing industries. *Poor Man's Rock*, probably the best and best known of the fifteen novels he published, is set in the Lasqueti Island area. The Great Depression brought hard times to magazine publishers and, as Sinclair's markets dried up, he augmented his income by fishing commercially. Sinclair enjoyed the camaraderie of the fishing fleet. To help pass the weather-bound, tied-up hours he sometimes read his stories and poems over the VHF radio. Sinclair died in Pender Harbour at the advanced age of 92, all but forgotten by the reading public, and his novels long out of print. "The Bank Trollers," given here in part, was a favourite.

The Bank Trollers[125]

. . . They ride the groundswell where grim Cape Cook
Thrusts to the west like a giant thumb,
They wallow abreast of Cape St. James
Past which the screaming nor'westers come.
The Horseshoe, Tow Hill, or far to the south
In the troubled waters of Nitinat's mouth.
Late in September they fish awhile
By foggy Swiftsure or Forty Mile,
'Till the fall southeasters drive them home
Chased by combers all white with foam;
Or over in Nawhitti where the strong tides flow —
All these are places the trollers know. . . .

124. For a biography of Sinclair see Betty C. Keller. *Pender Harbour Cowboy* (Victoria: TouchWood Editions, 2000).

125. Bertrand Sinclair, in *Raincoast Chronicles First Five* (Madiera Park: Harbour Publishing, 1976).

Driving shoreward in the dark of night
To drop his hood in some sheltered bight,
A lone wolf troller strains eyes and ears
For hazards that every seaman fears.
(No holy abbot of Aberthbrock
Has placed a bell on Bonilla Rock).
A freshening wind and a rising sea
Hammers the coastline under his lee.
Sudden he lifts on a great dark mound
That turns to white with a roaring sound.
A smash. Impaled on a sunken rock.
A second roller, a second shock.
Midships she bursts like an egg let fall
On a concrete walk. Her timbers all
Are riven, splintered, torn apart,
Stilled is the beat of her iron heart. . . .
In some distant anchorage, some safe bay,
When he writes his log at the close of day
Another troller will make this note:
"Lost, up Hecate, the fishing boat *Caricoa*
Seven ton. West coast troller. Crew of one."
Then he'll go below and put on the pot
And sip his coffee when it is hot,
Turn into his blankets and go to sleep,
Thinking of others still riding the deep.
Small wonder if now and then to him
The facts of life are a trifle grim.

Wind, fog, rain, on those offshore banks,
High-peaked groundswell or steep tide-rips,
While there's grub in the lockers and gas in the tanks,
The salmon trollers must make their trips.

Is there ease or glamour in this their life?
Ask any salmon troller's wife.
      — W. B. BERTRAND SINCLAIR

By 1920, over 100 canneries had been established along the West Coast.[126] The majority of the workers were Chinese who had been brought to the canneries by labour contractors with connections to Vancouver employment agencies. When Lily Chow delved into the history of the Chinese in BC, she came across records of the Chock On Agency. The collection included a poem written in Chinese by an unknown cannery worker. Lily Chow writes that kite flying was a favourite outdoor recreation and provides a translation of the poem.

Kite Song[127]

Though you are sailing
high up in the sky,
you are still held
in my hand.
Fly higher and float afar!
My beloved one
in distant land

would know
I am around
thinking of her,
when she sees
your beautiful wings
fluttering below the clouds.
                    — ANONYMOUS

126. Geoff. Meggs. *Salmon: the Decline of the BC Fishery* (Vancouver: Douglas & McIntyre, 1991).
127. Lily Chow, "The Chinese Canners in Port Essington," in *BC Historical News*, Spring 2001. Ms. Chow has also published two books: *Sojourners In the North* (Prince George: Caitlin Press, 1996) and *Chasing Their Dreams: Chinese Settlement in the Northwest Region of British Columbia* (Prince George: Caitlin Press, 2000).

Chinatown. At the dawn of the 1900s, the word evoked images of hidden passageways and tunnels, opium and gambling dens, slave girls, incense, and idolatry. One was well advised not to delve too deeply into this exotic Oriental world. However, one adventurous (and anonymous) scribe followed "with foreboding spirit" as his Chinese companion led him through Vancouver's Chinatown to a place called "The Shore of a Thousand Singing Shells." It was, he wrote, a place of enchantment: "From the blue ceiling hung jade-green and plum-coloured lanterns. The walls hid behind cherry-red and yellow hangings blazoned with flame-tongued dragons in bright gold, and figures of gods and men in wonderful costumes. Hangings swayed like gorgeous flowers in a long, wave-rhythmed dance of colour . . . Everything in the place had been brought from China, and there were . . . heavy aromas of burning prayer papers, incense sticks, opium and Chinese-made cigarettes. There were about a dozen Chinese in the room, and blue cobwebs of cigarette smoke swam among the soft-shining lanterns like ghosts of shredded dragons. The Chinese talked in the low voices of people speaking in the dark. I noticed that all wore queues and were in Chinese dress. Suddenly, with a frisking motion like that of a playful kitten, an ivory-tinted doll-like little slave girl in green trousers entered the room with a three-stringed guitar upon which she immediately picked some Chinese rag-time. The song was a ballad of love in a garden, and was old when the oldest of our songs were made. It is something like this:"[128]

Come Into the Garden, Lady

Lady mine, come into the garden.
The pearl moon is caught in the plum trees
like a kite
a soft breeze wafts sweet odors
from orchards pink with pear blossoms.

128. Edited from "Pieces of Eight," in *British Columbia* *Magazine*, August, 1911. p. 864.

Come into the garden, lady,
the black moth, Night, has opened her wings.
Come, lady of the flower feet,
night birds are singing
in the velvet dusk,
house lanterns are shining
like stars that drown
in the wine-dark water
of the star-reflecting lake,
the crystal bath
of the silver ducks.

Twenty years after its incorporation in 1886, Vancouver was still carving neighborhoods out of the surrounding wilderness. No longer a frontier village, its population tripled between 1900 and 1909. Construction was booming. A few automobiles rattled along downtown streets. Ladies wore long dresses and elaborate hats, and men donned starch-stiff collars and bowler hats.[129] In 1907, Vancouver resident M. P. Judge reflected on the city's progress.

Musings[130]

The vacant land was sold, and workmen cleared
Its undergrowth; their horses ploughed the earth:
With measurements the overseer marked
The outline of the houses soon to be.
And day by day long wooden scaffoldings
Grew higher, blocking out the distant view
Of mountains, sea, and sky, and open space, —
My window-world of morning, noon, and eve.

129. Bruce Macdonald. *Vancouver: A Visual History* (Vancouver: Talon Books, 1992).

130. M. P. Judge, in *Westward Ho! Magazine*. (Vancouver: British Columbia Magazine Co., December, 1907).

To others it may seem a little thing
To lose a view so loved, it seemed one's own;
I only know in having lost my view
I lose a friend behind the houses there.
The greatest loss has been the sunset hour,
The glory of the after-glow on sea,
And sky; the clouds that speak their loneliness
In radiant colour from the setting sun.
One consolation to myself I keep,
Is that I've had my view so long unclaimed,
And learnt so much in silence with the skies:
While in my heart live happy memories
Of dreaming moments by my window sit,
Where only good and far-off ideal thoughts
Dared muse with me in Nature's fairest moods.

    — M. P. JUDGE

TRANSMONTANUS is edited by Terry Glavin. Editorial correspondence should be sent to

Transmontanus
PO Box C25, Fernhill Road | Mayne Island, BC VON 2J0.

Published by New Star Books Ltd.
CANADA: 107 - 3477 Commercial Street | Vancouver, BC V5N 4E8
USA: 1574 Gulf Road, No. 1517 | Point Roberts, WA 98281
www.NewStarBooks.com | *info@NewStarBooks.com*

Edited for press by Melva McLean
Cover photograph: BC Archives
Cover by Rayola Graphic Design
Typesetting by New Star Books
Printed & bound in Canada by Imprimerie Gauvin
First printing June 2004

Publication of this work is made possible by grants from the Canada Council, the British Columbia Arts Council, and the Department of Canadian Heritage Book Publishing Industry Development Program.

NATIONAL LIBRARY OF CANADA CATALOGUING IN PUBLICATION DATA

The old red shirt : pioneer poets of British Columbia / [edited by] Yvonne Klan.

(Transmontanus ; 12)
Poems.
Includes bibliographical references.
ISBN 1-55420-006-7

1. Canadian poetry (English) — British Columbia.   2. Canadian poetry (English) — 19th century.   3. Canadian poetry (English) — 20th century.   I. Klan, Yvonne, 1930–   II. Series.
PS8295.5.B7043 2004   C811'.30809711   C2004-900788-2